Bond
No.1 for exam success

Maths
Word Problems

10 Minute Tests

CEM
(Durham University)

10–11+ years

OXFORD
UNIVERSITY PRESS

UNIVERSITY PRESS

Great Clarendon Street, Oxford, OX2 6DP, United Kingdom

Oxford University Press is a department of the University of Oxford.
It furthers the University's objective of excellence in research, scholarship,
and education by publishing worldwide. Oxford is a registered trade mark
of Oxford University Press in the UK and in certain other countries

Text © Oxford University Press 2017

Author: Michellejoy Hughes

The moral rights of the author have been asserted

First published in 2017

British Library Cataloguing in Publication Data
Data available

978-0-19-275940-5

10 9 8 7 6 5 4 3 2

Paper used in the production of this book is a natural, recyclable product
made from wood grown in sustainable forests. The manufacturing process
conforms to the environmental regulations of the country of origin.

Printed in China

Acknowledgements

Cover illustration: Lo Cole
Illustrations: Aptara
Page make-up: Aptara

Useful notes

How to do subtraction algebra

Example: $2a + 3b = 8$ $3a + 2b = 7$ Find the value of a and b.

1 Multiply the first equation by 3 and the second equation by 2:
$6a + 9b = 24$
$6a + 4b = 14$
2 Subtract the equations:
($6a - 6a$ cancels each other out, $9b - 4b = 5b$, $24 - 14 = 10$)
3 Solve the term b:
If $5b = 10$, then $b = 2$
4 Finally, replace b in either equation to find a:
$2a + 6 = 8$, so $a = 1$

How to do map scales

Example: My map scale is $1 : 750\,000$. What does 1 cm on the map represent?

1 First divide 750 000 by 100 to turn centimetres to metres.
2 Then divide 7500 by 1000 to turn metres to kilometres.
3 So 1 cm on the map represents 7.5 km in reality.

How to do common multiples

Example: Anna, Ben and Carol each have a bell to ring. Anna rings her bell every 3 seconds, Ben rings his bell every 4 seconds and Carol rings her bell every 5 seconds. In two minutes, how many times do they all ring their bells together?

1 A quick tip is to start with multiple knowledge. For example, all numbers in the 5 times table end in 0 or 5.
2 Select multiples of 3 that end in 0 or 5, up to 120: 15, 30, 45, 60, 75, 90, 105, 120
3 Select multiples of 4 that end in 0 or 5, up to 120: 20, 40, 60, 80, 100, 120
4 Look for the common numbers in both lists: 60, 120

In two minutes, they all ring their bells together twice.

How to do fraction logic

Example: I drove $\frac{3}{4}$ of a 200 km journey. How many kilometres have I driven?

1 Work out $\frac{1}{4}$ of 200 km (200 km $\div$ 4 = 50 km).
2 Calculate $\frac{3}{4}$ (50 km $\times$ 3 = 150 km).

Test 1

Matilda has read $\frac{1}{2}$ of the books that Sophia has read. Sophia has read $\frac{1}{4}$ of the books that Evie has read. Evie has read $\frac{2}{3}$ of the books that Daisy has read. Matilda has read seven books.

1 How many books has Daisy read?   _____ ☐ 1

2 How many books has Sophia read?   _____ ☐ 1

3 How many books were read by all of the girls?   _____ ☐ 1

> **Missing Numbers Tip!**
>
> Start with the number that you are given and then work backwards to find the answer.

Varni is using a function machine app. For every number that he enters into the app, the app will halve it, subtract six from the number and then multiply this number by three to find a total.

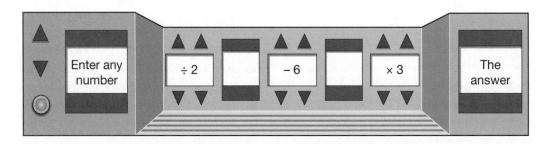

4 Varni enters the number 50. What answer will the app show?   _____ ☐ 1

5 Varni enters the number 120. What answer will the app show?   _____ ☐ 1

6 Varni enters the number 14. What answer will the app show?   _____ ☐ 1

Year 6 pupils created a chart to show the holiday destinations they had all been to during the year. Every child was included and they each went to just one destination. The pictogram shows how many pupils went to each destination. Each tick represents one pupil.

France	✓	✓	✓	✓	✓						
Wales	✓	✓	✓	✓	✓	✓	✓	✓	✓	✓	
Scotland	✓	✓	✓	✓	✓	✓					
England	✓	✓	✓	✓	✓	✓	✓	✓	✓	✓	✓
Greece	✓	✓	✓								
Portugal	✓	✓	✓	✓							
USA	✓	✓	✓								
Spain	✓	✓	✓	✓	✓	✓	✓	✓			

7 How many pupils were in Year 6? _____ ⬭1

8 What fraction of Year 6 went to Spain? _____ ⬭1

9 What percentage of the pupils went to England, Scotland or Wales? _____ ⬭1

Mr Rahman has a map with a scale of 1 : 150 000.

10 Mr Rahman travels 6 km from his home to the station. How many centimetres is this on the map? _____ ⬭1

11 He travels from the station to his friend's house which is 6 cm on the map. How many kilometres is this in real life? _____ ⬭1

Map Scale Tip!

The first number is the distance on the map and the second number is what this represents in real life, in centimetres. Divide the larger number by 100 to make metres, then by 1000 to make kilometres.

Total ⬚ 11

Test 2

Here is a section of a bus timetable. Use it to answer the following questions. Underline the correct answer for each question.

	Bus 1	Bus 2	Bus 3	Bus 4	Bus 5	Bus 6
Market	13:40	13:45	14:00	14:15	14:45	15:00
Shops	13:50	–	14:10	14:25	–	15:10
Church	13:58	–	14:18	14:33	–	15:18
Park	14:15	–	–	14:50	–	–
Leisure Centre	14:37	–	–	15:12	–	–
Beach	14:55	14:20	–	15:30	15:20	–
Bus Station	15:00	14:25	14:40	15:35	15:25	15:40

1 I get on the 13:40 bus from the market, get off at the church and then catch the next bus back to the bus station. What time do I reach the bus station?

    a 15:00   **b** 14:25   **c** 14:40   **d** 15:35   **e** 15:25

2 I want to get to the beach by 15:35. What is the latest bus I can catch from the market?

    a 13:40   **b** 13:45   **c** 14:00   **d** 14:15   **e** 14:45

3 What is the shortest time to get from the shops to the bus station?

    a 80 min   **b** 60 min   **c** 40 min   **d** 30 min   **e** 10 min

4 I reached the bus station at 15:40 after I had spent 1 hour and 20 minutes at the shops. What bus did I initially catch?

    a bus 1   **b** bus 2   **c** bus 3   **d** bus 4   **e** bus 6

5 Bus 7 has the same running time as Bus 1 and Bus 4. It leaves the market at 15:35. What time does it reach the bus station?

    a 16:40   **b** 16:45   **c** 16:50   **d** 16:55   **e** 17:00

Jasmine is making a fruit drink for Sports Day competitors. She needs to dilute the fruit juice with water in the ratio 1:5. Each carton of fruit juice contains 1 litre. Each glass will hold 300 millilitres and each of the 140 competitors will have one drink. Underline the correct answer for each question.

6 How much drink does Jasmine need to make?

a 1.5 litres   **b** 30 litres   **c** 42 litres   **d** 300 litres   **e** 420 litres

7 How much water does Jasmine need to use?

a 3 litres   **b** 5 litres   **c** 7.5 litres   **d** 35 litres   **e** 42 litres

8 How much fruit juice does Jasmine need to use?

a 3 litres   **b** 5 litres   **c** 7 litres   **d** 9 litres   **e** 11 litres

---

Ratio Tip!

When sharing an amount in a ratio, first add the parts in the ratio together; for example, to share £30 in a ratio of 1:2:3, add up 1 + 2 + 3 = 6. Next, divide this total into the amount given to find the value of one part (£30 ÷ 6 = £5). Finally, multiply one part by the original ratio numbers (£5 × 1; £5 × 2; £5 × 3).

Solomon buys a gift for his dad's birthday. Solomon buys a box that measures 35 cm × 28 cm × 12 cm to put the gift in. Solomon then buys some paper to cover the box. Underline the correct answer for each question.

9 What is the minimum amount of paper needed to cover the box?

a 75 cm^2 **b** 150 cm^2 **c** 11 760 cm^2 **d** 1736 cm^2 **e** 3472 cm^2

10 What is the total volume of the box?

a 75 cm^3 **b** 150 cm^3 **c** 11 760 cm^3 **d** 1736 cm^3 **e** 3472 cm^3

Total   10

Test 3

There are 390 pupils and 13 teachers at Westfield School. All of the teachers sit down at 4:00 p.m. and write 390 reports, taking the same time to write each one. They finish writing the reports at 6:30 p.m. Underline the correct answer for each question.

1 How long does it take each teacher to write one report?

    a 2.6 min   **b** 3.5 min   **c** 5 min   **d** 12 min   **e** 33.8 min

2 If three teachers were away, how long would it take the remaining teachers to write the reports?

    a 39 min   **b** 1 h 37.5 min   **c** 2 h 5 min   **d** 3 h 15 min   **e** 30 h

3 How long would it take six teachers to write the reports?

    a 26 min   **b** 2 h 42.5 min   **c** 3 h   **d** 3 h 15 min   **e** 5 h 25 min

---

At the art shop, paints cost £1.45 each, pencils cost £3.50 for a pack, and drawing pads cost £4.99 each or two for £8.

4 Eason buys four paints and two drawing pads. He pays with a £20 note.

How much change does Eason receive?   £ _____

5 The owner of the art shop remembers he is having a special event with 15% off the total bill.
How much extra change does Eason now receive?   £ _____

6 Eason's sister buys two paints, two packs of pencils and one drawing pad during the special event.
How much is her bill?   £ _____

7 Eason's brother buys a pack of pencils and pays with a £10 note.
The owner of the art shop gives him his change using the smallest number of coins possible.
How many coins does Eason's brother receive?   _____

Three apples and two pears have a mass of 630 g.

Two apples and three pears have a mass of 620 g.

The difference between the mass of one apple and the mass of one pear is 10 g.

8 What is the mass of one apple? _____ g

9 What is the mass of one pear? _____ g

> **Algebra Tip!**
>
> Don't forget to use the subtraction method to solve this type of question. Look back at the 'Useful notes' page if you need help in remembering this technique.

Aiden is making 120 gingerbread people. He decorates them in the following way.

- Every 2nd gingerbread person has eyes made from currants.
- Every 3rd gingerbread person has a white iced mouth.
- Every 5th gingerbread person has a liquorice nose.

Underline the correct answer for each question.

10 How many gingerbread people have a white iced mouth?

| a 15 | b 20 | c 30 | d 40 | e 60 |

11 How many gingerbread people have currant eyes and a liquorice nose?

| a 4 | b 12 | c 20 | d 55 | e 66 |

12 How many gingerbread people have currant eyes and a white iced mouth and a liquorice nose?

| a 4 | b 5 | c 6 | d 8 | e 12 |

Total 12

Test 4

Alfie has saved up money to put towards a new bike. He deposits £10 a month. Here is a graph of his bank account balance over 12 months. Use the graph to answer the following questions. Underline the correct answer for each question.

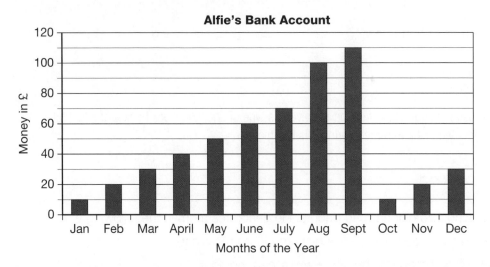

Alfie's Bank Account

1   When it was Alfie's birthday, he put extra money into his account. In which month was Alfie's birthday?

   a February   **b** May   **c** August   **d** October   **e** December

2   Alfie withdrew some money to put towards his bike. In which month did Alfie do this?

   a February   **b** May   **c** August   **d** October   **e** December

3   Alfie had already paid a 10% deposit on the bike. His dad then gave Alfie £80 so he had enough money to pay what he owed. How much was the full price of the bike?

   a £50   **b** £100   **c** £110   **d** £200   **e** £220

Evie bakes some cakes to sell at the cake bake stall. She spends £13.60 on ingredients that will make 80 cakes.

4   How much does Evie have to sell each cake for to cover the cost of the ingredients?   _____

5   Evie decides to sell her cakes for 40p each.
How much does she make in profit once her ingredient costs are
covered, if she sells all her cakes?   _____   ☐ 1

6   Evie sells 16 cakes to one customer.
What percentage of the total number of cakes is this?   _____   ☐ 1

The Dumfries Drummers have a new routine that lasts for 3 minutes. They divide
themselves into three groups.

Group A hit their drums every 2 seconds.

Group B hit their drums every 5 seconds.

Group C hit their drums every 7 seconds.

They all begin their performance at precisely 10:00 when they all hit their drums.

Underline the correct answer for each question.

7   How many times do groups A and B play their drums together in the new routine?   ☐ 1

   a   15   **b**   19   **c**   25   **d**   30   **e**   60

8   How many times do groups A and C play together in the new routine?   ☐ 1

   a   11   **b**   12   **c**   13   **d**   14   **e**   15

9   How many times do groups A, B and C all play their drums together in the
new routine?   ☐ 1

   a   3   **b**   4   **c**   5   **d**   6   **e**   7

10   The Dumfries Drummers lengthen the routine to a 5-minute performance.
How many times do groups A, B and C all play their drums together?   ☐ 1

   a   3   **b**   4   **c**   5   **d**   6   **e**   7

Total ☐ 10

Test 5

A group of Year 6 children conducted a survey of pupils' hair colour.

There were 180 children surveyed.

The hair colours were divided into dark, fair and red.

Twice as many children had dark hair than fair hair.

20% of the pupils had red hair.

1 How many pupils had dark hair?

   a 24   **b** 48   **c** 64   **d** 72   **e** 96

2 How many pupils had fair hair?

   a 24   **b** 48   **c** 64   **d** 72   **e** 96

3 How many pupils had red hair?

   a 9   **b** 18   **c** 20   **d** 36   **e** 40

Dara thinks that he knows a clever trick. He says,

"If you take one number that is one quarter of another number and add them together, they will always make a square number. When the same two numbers are multiplied together, they will also make a squared number. Any number with its 'quarter number' will always follow the same pattern."

4 Find a pair of numbers that seem to prove Dara's trick.   _____

5 Find a pair of numbers that disprove Dara's trick.   _____

> **Logic Tip!**
>
> With questions like this, always begin with an example number and work through systematically.
> Using low, easy numbers means that you can solve the equation in your head.

Zoe is putting some books back in the bookcase. There are seven books that are 17 cm, 13 cm, 28 cm, 20 cm, 32 cm, 12 cm and 25 cm tall. Zoe puts them in order of height. Underline the correct answer for each question.

6 How tall is the middle book?

a 28 cm   **b** 25 cm   **c** 20 cm   **d** 17 cm   **e** 13 cm

7 What is the mean height of the books?

a 19 cm   **b** 21 cm   **c** 24 cm   **d** 26 cm   **e** 32 cm

8 What is the range of the heights of the books?

a 20 cm   **b** 18 cm   **c** 15 cm   **d** 13 cm   **e** 10 cm

Beth is building a mini drone with a camera included.

9 The bottom panel of the drone is made from six triangles, each with a base of 5 cm and a height of 7 cm.
What is the area of the bottom panel?   _____

10 Beth then makes a carriage for the camera to sit in. The carriage has a length of 10 cm, a width of 8 cm and a height of 4 cm.
What is the volume of the carriage?   _____

11 Beth paints her drone in a specialised black and gold paint. She needs 15 ml of black paint and 30 ml of gold paint. Paint costs 63p for 5 ml.
How much does it cost Beth in paint?   _____

12 Beth attempts the first flight of the drone. It takes the drone 3 seconds to fly 2 metres.
If it flew at the same speed, how long would it take the drone to fly 12 metres?   _____

Total   12

Test 6

Mrs Fletcher is driving from Clun to Hay-on-Wye for lunch, which is a distance of 35 miles. After lunch she drives a further 40 miles to Ledbury. Underline the correct answer for each question.

1 Mrs Fletcher has driven 20% of her journey to Hay-on-Wye. How many miles has she driven?

   a 5   **b** 6   **c** 7   **d** 10   **e** 15

2 At 2:30 p.m., Mrs Fletcher has driven a total of 50 miles. What fraction of the day's driving has she done?

   a $\frac{1}{4}$ **b** $\frac{1}{3}$ **c** $\frac{1}{2}$ **d** $\frac{2}{3}$ **e** $\frac{3}{4}$

Yuri is digging a pond in his garden so that his pet ducks have somewhere to swim. He draws out a large rectangle on the ground so he knows where to begin digging.

Yuri draws a length of 12 m for the long side of the rectangle and then works out that the area of the rectangle is 48 m².

3 What is the length of the short side of the rectangle? _____

4 Yuri digs out the rectangle, digging to a depth of 2 m below the surface.

What is the total volume of the pond? _____

5 Yuri plants some reeds around the perimeter of the pond. The planting guide is 1 plant for every 50 cm.
How many plants does Yuri need? _____

Jack works in a travel agency, buying and selling foreign currency. Use his table of currency conversions on the opposite page to answer the following questions. Underline the correct answer for each question.

Currency	£1 is worth
Euro €	1.12
US dollar $	1.23
Indian rupee ₹	82.00

6 A customer is travelling to India and they want £100 worth of Indian rupees. How many Indian rupees will Jack give them?

   a 8.2   **b** 82   **c** 820   **d** 8200   **e** 82 000

7 A customer has returned from a holiday in the US and they have brought back $246. How many GB pounds will Jack return to them?

   a £2   **b** £20   **c** £200   **d** £2000   **e** £20 000

8 A customer wants €200. How much will this cost in GB pounds?

   a £112   **b** £152.43   **c** £178.57   **d** £224   **e** £2240

Rachel, Marion and Erica are sharing out 143 seeds to grow in the school vegetable patch. They share the seeds in the ratio 2 : 3 : 6. Underline the correct answer for each question.

9 How many seeds does Rachel have?

   a 15   **b** 26   **c** 39   **d** 78   **e** 100

10 How many seeds does Marion have?

   a 16   **b** 36   **c** 39   **d** 50   **e** 78

11 How many seeds does Erica have?

   a 26   **b** 68   **c** 72   **d** 78   **e** 85

Total 11

Test 7

Great Gaming Warehouse is having a sale. Games are reduced to £24.99 each with a 15% additional discount if you buy three games, **OR** a super 'Buy 4 get 1 free' offer.

1   Ellie buys her two favourite games. She pays with three £20 notes.
How much change does Ellie receive?   _____   [1]

2   Harry buys three games.
How much does he have to pay?   _____   [1]

3   Mr Hoskins wants ten games for presents for his grandchildren.
He buys the games in the cheapest way possible, and divides
the cost between his ten grandchildren.
How much does he spend on each grandchild?   _____   [1]

Here are the ingredients for Granny Khan's chocolate cupcakes. Use this list to answer the following questions. Underline the correct answer for each question.

Chocolate cupcakes (makes 12)

175 g of self-raising flour
175 g of butter or margarine
150 g of sugar
3 eggs
100 g of chocolate drops

4   Granny Khan makes 36 cupcakes. How many eggs does she use?   [1]

   a   3   **b**   4   **c**   6   **d**   9   **e**   12

5   Granny Khan makes 72 cupcakes. How much self-raising flour does she use?   [1]

   a   500 g   **b**   755 g   **c**   1050 g   **d**   1500 g   **e**   2000 g

6   Granny Khan has 100 g of sugar left. How many cupcakes can she make?   [1]

   a   6   **b**   7   **c**   8   **d**   9   **e**   10

Hashmee, Henry and Harry are all reading their books when they notice that the three books are all 96 pages long.

Hashmee says, "I've read $\frac{1}{3}$ of my book, so I've read the most."

Henry says, "I've read 25% of my book, so I've read the most."

Harry says, "I've only got 65 pages left to read, so I've read the most."

7 Which boy has read the most? _____ ⬭ 1

8 What is the mean number of pages the three boys have read? _____ ⬭ 1

The pupils at Lynton Junior School are going to dress up as their favourite book character. They were surveyed to find out what type of book character they wanted to dress as. Underline the correct answer for each question.

9 In Year 3, the most popular type of character was people from Roald Dahl books. 15 pupils, which was 30% of the year, wanted to dress up as a Roald Dahl character. How many pupils are in Year 3? ⬭ 1

    a 20   **b** 30   **c** 40   **d** 50   **e** 60

10 In Year 4, the most popular type of character was animals. Animals were preferred by 40% of the year, with 24 pupils choosing to dress up as animals. How many pupils are in Year 4? ⬭ 1

    a 30   **b** 40   **c** 50   **d** 60   **e** 70

11 In Year 5, the most popular type of character was people from history. 20 pupils chose to dress up as historical figures, which was 25% of the year. How many pupils are in Year 5? ⬭ 1

    a 40   **b** 50   **c** 60   **d** 70   **e** 80

12 In Year 6, the most popular type of character was superheroes. 18 pupils, which was 15% of the year, chose superheroes as their preferred character type. How many pupils are in Year 6? ⬭ 1

    a 30   **b** 60   **c** 90   **d** 120   **e** 150

Total ⬭ 12

Test 8

A new television channel is running a survey on the most popular types of children's programmes. Here are their results:

Television Programmes

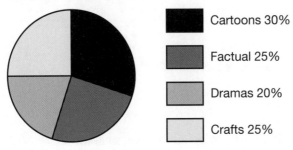

Cartoons 30%

Factual 25%

Dramas 20%

Crafts 25%

40 children preferred factual programmes. Use the pie chart to answer the following questions.

1 How many children took part in the survey? _____ ☐ 1

2 How many children preferred cartoons? _____ ☐ 1

3 How many fewer children preferred dramas than cartoons? _____ ☐ 1

> ### Pie Chart Tip!
> Remember your percentages in these questions: 25% will look like a quarter of a circle, 50% will look like half a circle.

Juliet has a map with a scale of 1 : 250 000.

4 Juliet is travelling to the beach for a picnic. On the map, the beach measures 7 cm from her house.
How many kilometres is the beach from her house? _____ ☐ 1

5 Juliet then drives 24 km from the beach to her mum's house.
How many centimetres is this on the map? _____ ☐ 1

Min, Noah and Peter have some stickers.

m = number of stickers Min has to start with

n = number of stickers Noah has to start with

p = number of stickers Peter has to start with

Look at the following expressions and match them to the scenarios below. Underline the correct answer for each question.

6 Noah gives eight stickers to Min. How many stickers does Noah have now?

a $n - 8$ **b** $m + 8$ **c** $8n$ **d** $8m$ **e** $\frac{n}{8}$

7 Peter gives Min five stickers. How many stickers does Min have now?

a $p - m$ **b** $m + 13$ **c** $13m$ **d** $5mp$ **e** $\frac{p}{5}$

8 Min, Noah and Peter add their stickers together and then they share them equally. How many stickers do they each have?

a mnp **b** $m + n + p$ **c** $(m + n + p) \div 3$ **d** $(m + n + p) \times 3$ **e** $3mnp$

Years 3, 4, 5 and 6 at Corfton School have been presented with some new classroom books in the ratio $1:2:3:4$.

In total, 2500 books were presented to the school.

60% of the books given to each year were paperback and the rest were hardback.

70% of both types of books given to each year were fiction and the rest were factual.

9 How many books does Year 3 have?   _____

10 How many paperback books does Year 4 have?   _____

11 How many fiction books does Year 5 have?   _____

12 How many hardback, factual books does Year 6 have?   _____

Total   12

Test 9

A 5 kg bag of flour costs £3.40, a 1 kg bag of flour costs £1.80, a 750 g bag of flour costs £1.40 and a 500 g bag of flour costs 95p.

1 Which size bag of flour costs the least per kilogram? _____ 1

2 Which size bag of flour costs the most per kilogram? _____ 1

Wilton School wanted to know which vegetables pupils preferred at lunchtime. Use the pictogram of their survey results to answer the following questions. Underline the correct answer for each question.

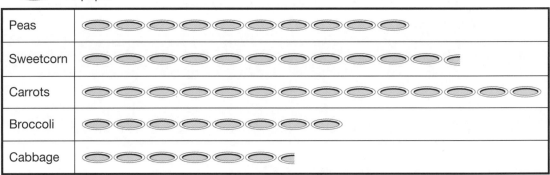

= 10 pupils

3 How many more pupils preferred sweetcorn than cabbage? 1

   a 55   **b** 50   **c** 45   **d** 40   **e** 35

4 What percentage of pupils preferred peas? 1

   a 10%   **b** 20%   **c** 30%   **d** 40%   **e** 50%

5 What fraction of pupils voted for carrots? 1

   a $\frac{7}{10}$ **b** $\frac{7}{15}$ **c** $\frac{7}{18}$ **d** $\frac{7}{20}$ **e** $\frac{7}{25}$

Some Year 6 pupils are looking for patterns in nature.

6 Emily is counting snowflakes as they land on the window and she recognises that they are making a sequence.
The sequence begins like this: 1, 2, 3, 5, 8, 13
What would the 10th number of her sequence be? _____

7 As the snowdrops melt, Tom counts the drips as they run down the window.
He recognises that they are making a sequence.
The sequence begins like this: 1, 1, 2, 4, 7, 11
What would the 12th number of his sequence be? _____ ◯1

8 When the melted snow drips, it forms puddles. Grace measures the length of the puddles and recognises that they are making a sequence.
The sequence begins like this: 6, 7, 12, 14, 18, 21
What would the 13th number of her sequence be? _____ ◯1

Sequences Tip!

The quickest way to solve a sequence is to jot down the difference between consecutive numbers so that you can visualise any patterns.

Malachi is trying to work out the mass of some items. This is what he knows:
- 3 magnets and 4 blocks of metal have a mass of 1000 g
- 4 magnets and 5 blocks of metal have a mass of 1280 g

Malachi writes down the information as two equations:

$3m + 4b = 1000\,g$ $\qquad 4m + 5b = 1280\,g$

Underline the correct answer for each question.

9 What is the mass of one magnet?

   a 120 g   **b** 125 g   **c** 130 g   **d** 150 g   **e** 160 g

10 What is the mass of one block of metal? ◯1

   a 120 g   **b** 140 g   **c** 160 g   **d** 180 g   **e** 200 g

Total ◯10

Test 10

The toy shop is organising the items that it sells. They find the following:

- There are 45 jigsaws on the top shelves.
- There are 30 dolls and teddy bears on the middle shelves.
- There are 55 boxes of building kits on the lower shelves.
- There are 20 board games in the window display.

1 What percentage of the items are dolls and teddy bears?   _____   ☐ 1

2 What fraction of the items are jigsaws?   _____   ☐ 1

Mo is selling phone cases. They cost him 60p each to buy and he sells them for £1 each or four for £3. Underline the correct answer for each question.

3 Mo has £20 to buy as many phone cases as possible. What is the maximum amount of profit that he can make once he has recovered the cost of buying them?   ☐ 1

  a £5   **b** £11   **c** £13   **d** £14   **e** £33

4 Mo buys 120 phone cases. How many does he need to sell individually at £1 each before he starts making a profit?   ☐ 1

  a 30   **b** 40   **c** 60   **d** 72   **e** 120

5 Mo buys 200 phone cases and sells them all in bundles of four. What is the maximum amount of profit that he can make once he has recovered the cost of buying them?   ☐ 1

  a £8   **b** £10   **c** £13   **d** £30   **e** £50

A map has a scale of 1 : 640 000.

6 Bob is going to the station. He has to travel 1.6 km to get there.

How many centimetres is this on the map?   _____   ☐ 1

7 Joy is travelling to the coast at the weekend. On the map this measures 24 cm.

How many kilometres will she be travelling? _____ ⬭ 1

8 Dot is flying to Scotland for a business meeting. She has already travelled 450 km and is $\frac{2}{3}$ of the way through her journey.

How far will she have travelled when she completes her journey? _____ ⬭ 1

Here are the scores from a maths test that some Year 6 pupils completed. The total scores were out of 20. Use the table to answer the following questions. Underline the correct answer for each question.

Name	Score
Brin	17
Fred	18
Heber	20
Simeon	16
Squire	19

9 What was the mean score? ⬭ 1

   a 16   **b** 17   **c** 18   **d** 19   **e** 20

10 Who scored the same as the median score? ⬭ 1

   a Brin   **b** Fred   **c** Heber   **d** Simeon   **e** Squire

11 What was the range of the scores? ⬭ 1

   a 1   **b** 2   **c** 3   **d** 4   **e** 5

Finding Averages Tip!

To find the mean, add up the scores and then divide by the total number of scores. To find the median, put the scores in order and choose the middle score. To find the range, subtract the lowest score from the highest score.

Total   11

Sandy Beach Café has a chart of the most popular items throughout the week.
Use the chart for last week to answer the following questions.

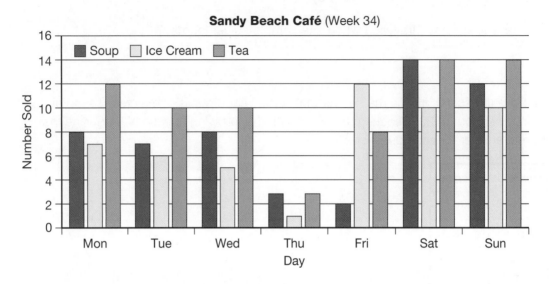

Sandy Beach Café (Week 34)

1 Which day of the week did it rain heavily? _____ ⬭1

2 Which day was the busiest? _____ ⬭1

3 How many cups of tea were sold over the week? _____ ⬭1

There are 184 pupils in Year 6. They are all going on a half-day school trip to the
museum with eight teachers. Each coach can carry 56 people and costs £175 to hire
for half a day. Entrance to the museum is £1.75 each.

4 How many coaches are needed to transport everyone
to the museum? _____ ⬭1

5 What is the total cost for the coach hire and the museum fee? _____ ⬭1

6 If everyone pays the same for the coach, how much does
each person pay for the coach fare and museum cost?
Remember to round your answer up or down. _____ ⬭1

A café is creating an extension 24 m long by 24 m wide. Each table and chair space measures 2 metres long by 2 metres wide. There must be a walkway of at least 2 metres around every table for people to move about and a 2-metre gap between each table and the wall. Underline the correct answer for each question.

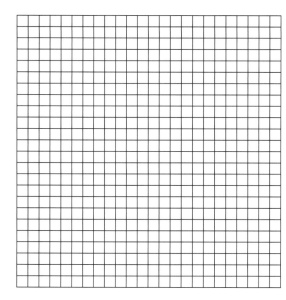

Each grid square is 1 m × 1 m

☐ = 2 m × 2 m table and chair

7 What is the maximum number of tables that will fit into an extension 24 metres by 24 metres?

| 1 |

a 25 **b** 36 **c** 49 **d** 64 **e** 144

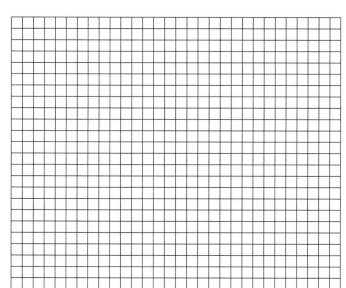

Each grid square is 1 m × 1 m

☐ = 2 m × 2 m table and chair

8 How many tables will fit into an extension 24 metres long by 30 metres wide?

| 1 |

a 26 **b** 30 **c** 35 **d** 36 **e** 40

Total | 8

Test 12

Jas is making some magnetic monster models. He uses heads, bodies, eyes and legs in the ratio $1:1:3:5$ with each model having one head.

1   Jas has 20 heads, 20 bodies, 20 eyes and 20 legs.
What is the maximum number of models that Jas can make?   _____   [1]

2   Jas has 24 heads, 17 bodies, 28 eyes and 31 legs.
What is the maximum number of models that Jas can make?   _____   [1]

3   Jas wants to make 16 models. Fill in the numbers in this sentence:

Jas needs _____ heads, _____ bodies, _____ eyes

and _____ legs.   [1]

Alice rolls two 1–6 dice together once and makes a note of the total score rolled.
Underline the correct answer for each question.

4   What is the probability that Alice will roll a single digit score?   [1]

a $\frac{5}{6}$ **b** $\frac{2}{3}$ **c** $\frac{1}{2}$ **d** $\frac{1}{3}$ **e** $\frac{1}{6}$

5   What is the probability that Alice will roll a prime number?   [1]

a $\frac{1}{6}$ **b** $\frac{1}{4}$ **c** $\frac{1}{3}$ **d** $\frac{5}{12}$ **e** $\frac{1}{2}$

6   What is the probability that Alice will roll a square number?   [1]

a $\frac{1}{12}$ **b** $\frac{1}{9}$ **c** $\frac{5}{36}$ **d** $\frac{1}{6}$ **e** $\frac{7}{36}$

> **Probability Tip!**
> Making an outcomes table to show the possible scores is an effective way of solving probability problems with dice or with coins.

Beth is walking from her home to the library. She has walked for 6 minutes and has walked $\frac{3}{5}$ of the way. Underline the correct answer for each question.

7 How long will it take Beth to walk all of the way to the library?

    a 7 min   **b** 8 min   **c** 9 min   **d** 10 min   **e** 12 min

8 If Beth walks at 5 kilometres per hour, how far is the library from her home?

    a 800 m   **b** 833 m   **c** 868 m   **d** 883 m   **e** 898 m

9 One week Beth walks from her home to the library and back on six days. She maintains her speed of 5 kilometres per hour. How far does Beth walk that week? Round your answer to the nearest kilometre.

    a 0.5 km   **b** 1 km   **c** 2 km   **d** 5 km   **e** 10 km

Jet sells packs of soap in his pharmacy. There are 64 packs of soap in each box and there are 25 boxes in a pallet. Jet buys two pallets. He pays £1024 in total for his soap and he sells each pack of soap for £2.50. Underline the correct answer for each question.

10 How many packs of soap does Jet buy?

    a 178   **b** 1200   **c** 1600   **d** 2400   **e** 3200

11 How many packs of soap does Jet have to sell before he is able to make any profit?

    a 409   **b** 410   **c** 412   **d** 414   **e** 416

12 What is the maximum profit that Jet can make?

    a £2176   **b** £3200   **c** £4800   **d** £6976   **e** £8000

13 Jet decides to sell the soap in sets of three packs for £5 a set. What is the maximum profit to the nearest pound that Jet can now make?

    a £2133   **b** £4306   **c** £5333   **d** £6033   **e** £8000

Total 13

Test 13

Here is part of a bus timetable:

Bus route	464	512	689
Station	13:45	13:50	14:00
Market	13:58	–	14:13
Church	14:04	–	–
Shops	14:14	14:08	14:23

1 Dahnis is meeting his friend at the shops at quarter past two.
What is the latest he can leave the station to get there in time? _____ [1]

2 Zara catches the 464 bus from the station and gets off at the market. Then she
catches the next bus from the market and gets off at the shops.
What time does Zara reach the shops? _____ [1]

3 What is the quickest time between the market and the shops? _____ [1]

Michael, Brooke and Stanley have 180 stickers shared equally between them. Michael
gives Brooke $\frac{1}{4}$ of his stickers. Brooke gives 30% of her original stickers to Stanley.
Stanley gives Michael 20% of his original stickers. Underline the correct answer for
each question.

4 How many stickers does Michael now have? [1]

   a 70   b 68   c 60   d 57   e 55

5 How many stickers does Brooke now have? [1]

   a 70   b 68   c 60   d 57   e 55

6 How many stickers does Stanley now have? [1]

   a 70   b 66   c 60   d 57   e 55

The accounts department at S J Trading has worked out exactly how much the company has made over the past year. The exact sum is £172 496.36 but other departments only need a rough guide.

7 How much is this to the nearest thousand pounds? _____ ⬚ 1

8 How much is this to the nearest hundred pounds? _____ ⬚ 1

9 How much is this to the nearest ten thousand pounds? _____ ⬚ 1

10 How much is this to the nearest hundred thousand pounds? _____ ⬚ 1

Rounding Tip!

Remember, when rounding numbers up and down, you need to look at the digit to the **RIGHT** of the number placement needed. Don't forget to write the correct number of zeros so that all the digits are in the correct place value column.

Peter has four pieces of card with a number written on each. Sean also has four pieces of card with a number written on each. All of the numbers are whole numbers and all are less than the number 15. Peter and Sean pick one card each. Peter adds the two numbers together and Sean multiplies the two numbers together. Then they put their two answers side by side to make a four-digit code.

11 Which two numbers are added and then multiplied to make the code 1984? _____ ⬚ 1

12 Which two numbers are added and then multiplied to make the code 1544? _____ ⬚ 1

13 Which two numbers are added and then multiplied to make the code 1639? _____ ⬚ 1

14 Which two numbers are added and then multiplied to make the code 1130? _____ ⬚ 1

Total ⬚ 14

Test 14

Here is a temperature guide for today. Use the table to answer the following questions.

City, Country	°C
Anchorage, Alaska	−9
Baghdad, Iraq	32
Helsinki, Finland	5
Khartoum, Sudan	39
London, UK	14
Moscow, Russia	−2
Mumbai, India	28
Tokyo, Japan	17

1 What is the difference between the lowest and the highest temperatures? _____ ☐1

2 What is the mean temperature of the hottest three cities? _____ ☐1

3 What is the mean temperature of the coldest three cities? _____ ☐1

4 How much warmer is Baghdad than Anchorage? _____ ☐1

If a book is returned to the library late, there is a charge in pence. The formula the library uses for each book is $C = 10d$ where C is the **cost in pence**, and d is the **number of days overdue**.

5 Louisa has returned four books 2 days late.
How much is she charged? _____

6 Kayleigh has returned one book 1 week late.
How much is she charged? _____

7 Jodie has returned three books 2 weeks late. She pays with a £10 note. How much change does she receive? _____

A clothes shop has a sale on. All prices are reduced. Underline the correct answer for each question.

8 Vijay buys two shirts that were £25 each but have been reduced by 30%. How much does Vijay pay in total?

   a £15   b £30   c £35   d £40   e £42

9 Vijay buys a pair of jeans for £32.50. The original price was £50. By what percentage were the jeans reduced?

   a 5%   b 15%   c 25%   d 35%   e 45%

Percentages Tip!

Working out 10% by simply dividing by 10 is a great way to quickly solve these percentage questions. Once you have 10%, it is simple to find multiples of 10% or to halve to find 5%.

Ben is making a triangular sail for his model yacht. The height of the sail is 38 cm and the base of the sail is 18 cm. Ben has a piece of material that is 40 cm wide and 40 cm long.

10 Ben cuts out his triangular sail.
What area of material is left over? _____

11 Ben is going to attach his sail to the boom of his model yacht. The base of the sail is 18 cm and Ben needs to punch one hole every 36 mm.
How many holes will he need to punch? _____

12 Ben has to tie a piece of thread through each hole that is then tied to the boom. Ben has 37.5 cm of thread that he needs to divide equally between each hole. How long is each piece of thread that he cuts? _____

Test 15

Caleb has a biscuit machine. He can put in portions of dough and the machine will then produce the number of biscuits following the functions.

Here are the three programmes that Caleb uses the most:

	Function 1	Function 2
Programme 1	× 3	+ 12
Programme 2	+ 8	× 3
Programme 3	× 4	+ 20

1 Caleb puts three portions of dough into programme 2.
How many biscuits will this produce? _____ ⬭1

2 Caleb puts 12 portions of dough into programme 3.
How many biscuits will this produce? _____ ⬭1

3 Caleb puts 15 portions of dough into programme 1.
How many biscuits will this produce? _____ ⬭1

Philip's train was due at 5:56 p.m., but it was running late by 12 minutes.

4 What time did Philip's train arrive in 24-hour time? _____ ⬭1

5 Philip's watch was running fast by 3 minutes.
When the train arrived, what was the time on Philip's watch in 24-hour time? _____ ⬭1

6 Philip then had a 20-minute walk home, but he stopped at the shop first and spent 8 minutes shopping.
What was the time on Philip's watch when he returned home? _____ ⬭1

Morgan has a map with a scale of 1 : 45 000.

7 Morgan is travelling from home to the leisure centre. On the map, this journey measures 5 cm.
How far is this in real life? _____ ◯ 1

8 Morgan is then going from the railway station to visit her grandparents. They live 6 km away.
How many centimetres is this on the map? _____ ◯ 1

The petting zoo has some new rabbits. Abinaath measures the rabbits' height and mass and records the details. Use his table of results to answer the following questions. Underline the correct answer for each question.

Rabbit	Flopsy	Tipsy	Fluffy	Tufty	Colin
Height	6 cm	9 cm	5 cm	8 cm	7 cm
Mass	45 g	100 g	65 g	110 g	85 g

9 What is the mean height of the rabbits? ◯ 1

   a 5 cm   **b** 6 cm   **c** 7 cm   **d** 8 cm   **e** 9 cm

10 What is the mean mass of the rabbits? ◯ 1

   a 58 g   **b** 65 g   **c** 72 g   **d** 81 g   **e** 93 g

11 What is the range of the rabbits' masses? ◯ 1

   a 58 g   **b** 65 g   **c** 72 g   **d** 81 g   **e** 93 g

12 What is the range of the rabbits' heights? ◯ 1

   a 2 cm   **b** 3 cm   **c** 4 cm   **d** 5 cm   **e** 6 cm

Total ⬜ 12

Test 16

Madison is always borrowing money, so her dad is teaching her how to budget. She can borrow as much as she wants, but she has to pay him back 10% of the loan every day for the amount she owes. If she cannot pay the money back the next day, she then owes the amount borrowed, the 10% from the previous day and then another 10% of this total sum. Underline the correct answer for each question.

1   Madison borrows £20 on the 3rd December and pays it back on the 6th December. How much does she have to give back to her dad?

   a £20.30   **b** £22.00   **c** £24.20   **d** £26.00   **e** £26.62

2   Madison borrows £10 on Saturday and pays it back on Tuesday. How much does she have to give back to her dad?

   a £10.40   **b** £11.00   **c** £13.00   **d** £13.31   **e** £30.00

3   At the end of the month Madison borrows some money for 2 days and pays her dad back the sum of £9.68. How much did Madison borrow?

   a £6.00   **b** £7.00   **c** £8.00   **d** £9.00   **e** £10.00

George is working on a jigsaw puzzle. He has completed $\frac{3}{5}$ of a 720-piece jigsaw. Underline the correct answer for each question.

4   How many pieces of the jigsaw has George already put in place?

   a 144   **b** 288   **c** 432   **d** 516   **e** 612

5   George completes the jigsaw over the next two evenings, putting the same number of pieces in place on both evenings. How many pieces does he add to the puzzle each evening?

   a 72   **b** 144   **c** 216   **d** 240   **e** 480

6 George spends exactly 2.5 hours on each of the next two evenings on the jigsaw puzzle. What is his mean speed in pieces per hour?

a 96   **b** 62   **c** 58   **d** 56   **e** 52

Merry has bought a new box of building blocks for her brother's birthday. The box measures 75 cm long, 60 cm wide and 35 cm tall.

7 What is the surface area of the box? _____

8 Merry has a roll of wrapping paper that is 3 m long and 1 m wide. Will it be big enough to wrap the present? _____

9 What is the volume of the building blocks box? Give your answer in m³. _____

> **Converting Volume Tip!**
>
> Here you need to find the answer in m³. Convert the measurements given in the question from centimetres to metres before multiplying to find the volume. Alternatively, work out the volume in centimetres and then convert from cm³ to m³ by dividing the answer by 100 for each dimension, or 1 000 000 in total; this is the same as dividing by 10 six times.

Nick needs some winter clothes from the shop.
He buys some gloves, which cost £8.
He buys a hat, which costs £10.
He buys a scarf, which costs £14.
The shop has a 15% sale on.

10 How much do the gloves, hat and scarf come to before the discount? _____

11 How much does Nick pay once the discount has been taken off? _____

12 Nick pays with two £20 pound notes. How much change does he receive? _____

Total 12

Test 17

Jo has recorded the travelling that she did last Saturday on a distance–time graph. Use her graph to answer the following questions. Underline the correct answer for each question.

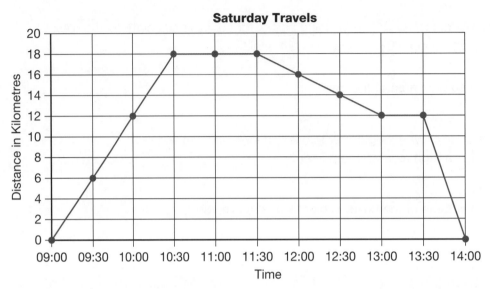

1 At 9 a.m., Jo travelled by bus to her dad's house. How far was her dad's house in kilometres?

a 10 km   **b** 12 km   **c** 14 km   **d** 16 km   **e** 18 km

2 Jo stayed at her dad's house. How long did Jo spend at her dad's house?

a $\frac{1}{2}$ hour   **b** 1 hour   **c** $1\frac{1}{2}$ hour   **d** 2 hours   **e** $2\frac{1}{2}$ hours

3 Jo's dad drove her home but they stopped for half an hour for lunch. What time did they begin their lunch break?

a 10:30   **b** 11:00   **c** 12:00   **d** 13:00   **e** 13:30

Austin has some counters in a bag. He has 27 white counters, 17 green counters, 14 red counters and 12 blue counters. Underline the correct answer for each question.

4 What is the probability that Austin will draw out a red counter?

a 5%   **b** 10%   **c** 15%   **d** 20%   **e** 25%

5 What is the probability that Austin will draw out a white or a blue counter?

 a $\frac{3}{7}$ **b** $\frac{33}{70}$ **c** $\frac{39}{70}$ **d** $\frac{4}{7}$ **e** $\frac{3}{4}$

Mr Preston buys some books from a bookshop where they are having a sale.
He purchases three books which cost £5, £10 and £12.

6 Mr Preston can buy two books at full price and get the third, cheapest book for free.
How much would this cost him?   _____

7 Instead of using this first offer, Mr Preston can have 25% off the original £27 cost of the three books.
How much would the books cost him using this discount?   _____

8 Mr Preston chooses the cheaper deal and pays with two £20 notes.
How much change does he get back?   _____

Trevor is working out the mass of some items. He places different combinations of items on the scales and weighs them. He then tries to work out the mass of individual items.

= 737 g   = 450 g

= 447 g   = 344 g

What is the mass of each of the following items?

9 _____   **11** _____

10 _____   **12** _____

13 What is the mean mass of the four different items?   _____

Total   13

Test 18

Here is a diagram of Mrs Basley's back garden. Use it to answer the following questions.

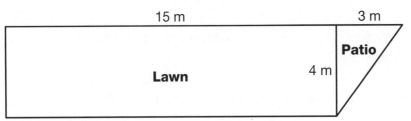

15 m   3 m

Patio

Lawn   4 m

1 What is the total area of the lawn and patio?   _____   1

2 How many times larger is the lawn than the patio?   _____   1

3 Mrs Basley uses 145 stones to edge the lawn. Each stone costs £1.82 with a 20% discount if she spends over £100. Delivery costs £20 or is free if she spends over £275.

What is the total price Mrs Basley pays for 145 stones with delivery?_____   1

Pretty Pooch Parlour has five dogs in for a wash. Use the details in the table to answer the following questions. Underline the correct answer for each question.

Dog	Mass
Twinkle	32 kg
Teddy Bear	60 kg
Biffo	16 kg
Smokey	48 kg
Pippi	4 kg

4 What is the mean mass of the five dogs?   1

   a 25 kg   **b** 30 kg   **c** 32 kg   **d** 35 kg   **e** 40 kg

5 If the dogs were lined up in order of mass, which would be the middle dog?   1

   a Twinkle   **b** Teddy Bear **c** Biffo   **d** Smokey   **e** Pippi

Test continues after Answers section →

Answers

Test 1

(pages 4–5)

1–3 Start with the Matilda who has read 7 books. Matilda has read $\frac{1}{2}$ of the books Sophia has read, so Sophia has read $7 \times 2 = 14$ books.

14 is $\frac{1}{4}$ of the books that Evie has read, so Evie has read $14 \times 4 = 56$ books.

This is $\frac{2}{3}$ of the number of books Daisy has read, so Daisy has read $56 \times 3 \div 2 = 84$ books.

1 Daisy: 84 books

2 Sophia: 14 books

3 161 books read by all the girls $(7 + 14 + 56 + 84 = 161)$

4 57 $(50 \div 2 = 25; 25 - 6 = 19; 19 \times 3 = 57)$

5 162 $(120 \div 2 = 60; 60 - 6 = 54; 54 \times 3 = 162)$

6 3 $(14 \div 2 = 7; 7 - 6 = 1; 1 \times 3 = 3)$

7 50 pupils $(5 + 10 + 6 + 11 + 3 + 4 + 3 + 8 = 50)$

8 $\frac{4}{25}$ (8 children out of 50 children went to Spain; $\frac{8}{50}$. When working with fractions, remember to give your answer in its simplest form. $\frac{8}{50}$ is equivalent to $\frac{4}{25}$)

9 54% (Add up the numbers of pupils going to England, Scotland and Wales: $11 + 6 + 10 = 27$ pupils. There is a total of 50 pupils. $\frac{27}{50}$ went to England, Scotland or Wales. To find a percentage, you need the denominator to be 100; here you can double the numerator and denominator to find the equivalent fraction $\frac{54}{100}$. Once you have a fraction with 100 as the denominator, you have the percentage. $\frac{54}{100} = 54\%$)

10–11 The scale of 1 : 150 000 means that 1 cm on the map represents 150 000 cm in reality. Dividing 150 000 cm by 100 (to make 1500 metres) and then by 1000 (to make 1.5 km), makes it easier to solve these problems. 1 cm is equivalent to 1.5 km.

You can now scale up or down using this information: if 1 cm is equivalent to 1.5 km then 2 cm is equivalent to 3 km, 4 cm is equivalent to 6 km, etc. You can also work this in reverse: if 1.5 km is equivalent to 1 cm, then 3 km is equivalent to 2 cm and 6 km is equivalent to 4 cm.

10 4 cm (If 1.5 km is represented by 1 cm, then 6 km is represented by 4 cm (6 km ÷ 1.5 km = 4))

11 9 km (If 1 cm is equivalent to 1.5 km, then 6 cm is equivalent to 9 km (1.5 km × 6 = 9 km))

Test 2

(pages 6–7)

1 c (I get the 13:40 bus from the market, get off at 13:58 at the church. The next bus to the bus station leaves at 14:18, getting to the bus station at 14:40)

2 e (Buses 4 and 5 would both get me there on time, but Bus 5 leaves at the later time of 14:45 and gets to the beach at 15:20)

3 d (Buses 1 and 4 would both take 1 hour and 10 minutes. Buses 2 and 5 do not visit the shops. Therefore Buses 3 and 6 take the shortest time, which is 30 minutes)

4 a (Bus 6 reaches the bus station at 15:40, so this is the bus I caught from the shops. Bus 6 left the shops at 15:10. I spent 1 hour and 20 minutes at the shops so I must have arrived 1 hour 20 minutes earlier. 15:10 minus 1 hour is 14:10, minus 20 minutes is 13:50. Bus 1 arrived at the shops at 13:50)

5 d (Bus 1 takes 1 hour and 20 minutes to travel from the market to the bus station. If bus 7 leaves the market at 15:35 it will reach the bus station at 15:35 plus 1 hour 20 minutes, which is 16:55)

6–8 A table like this can be useful for this type of question:

Fruit juice	Water	Total drink
1	5	6
2	10	12
3	15	18
4	20	24
5	25	30
6	30	36
7	35	42

For every 1 litre of fruit juice Jasmine needs 5 litres of water. This makes 6 litres of drink (1 litre of fruit juice + 5 litres of water).

There are 140 competitors and each glass holds 300 ml, so Jasmine needs to make 42 000 ml of drink (140 competitors × 300 ml). Divide 42 000 by 1000 to convert from millilitres to litres (there are 1000 ml in 1 litre); 42 000 ÷ 1000 = 42 litres of drink needed in total. To find out how much fruit juice and water is needed, divide 42 litres by 6 litres; 42 ÷ 6 = 7. This means that Jasmine needs 7 × 1 litre = 7 litres of fruit juice and 7 × 5 litres = 35 litres of water.

6 c (300 ml × 140 competitors = 42 000 ml or 42 litres)

7 d (7 × 5 litres = 35 litres)

8 c (7 × 1 litre = 7 litres)

9 e (Surface area means the area of the six faces: the top and bottom, the left side and the right side, the front and the back. To cover the surface area of the box, Solomon needs (35 cm × 28 cm × 2) + (28 cm × 12 cm × 2) + (35 cm × 12 cm × 2) = 3472 cm². Note: If Solomon were going to *wrap* the box up, he would need more paper. This is because wrapping a present would require sufficient paper to fold over and stick together)

10 c (Volume means multiplying the three dimensions together; 35 cm × 28 cm × 12 cm = 11 760 cm³)

Test 3

(pages 8–9)

1–3 It takes 13 teachers 2.5 hours to write the reports so 13 × 2.5 = 32.5 total teacher hours to write all of the reports. To find a time per report, divide the total time (32.5 hours = 1950 minutes) by the 390 pupils; 1950 ÷ 390 = 5 minutes per report.

1 c (5 minutes is the time taken by each teacher to write one report)

2 d (1950 minutes ÷ 10 teachers = 195 minutes, or 3 hours 15 minutes)

3 e (1950 minutes ÷ 6 teachers = 325 minutes or 5 hours 25 minutes)

4 £6.20 (Two drawing pads cost £8. Four paints cost 4 × £1.45 = £5.80. Four paints and two drawing pads cost £5.80 + £8 = £13.80. The amount of change received is £20 − £13.80 which equals £6.20)

5 £2.07 (He gets 15% off £13.80; 10% of £13.80 is £1.38; 5% of £13.80 is half of 10% = £0.69; extra change = £1.38 + £0.69 = £2.07)

6 £12.66 (£1.45 × 2 for two paints + £3.50 × 2 for two packs of pencils + £4.99 for one drawing pad = £14.89; 10% of £14.89 = £1.489; 5% of £14.89 = £0.7445; 15% of £14.89 = £2.2335; £14.89 − £2.2335 = £12.6565 (rounds to £12.66))

7 4 coins (£10 − £3.50 = £6.50. The smallest number of coins that can be used to make £6.50 is 4: 50p + £2 + £2 + £2)

8–9 Use the equations $3a + 2p = 630$ and $2a + 3p = 620$ to represent the problem. There are two terms in each equation, a (mass of one apple), p (mass of one pear). To make the a term the same in both equations, multiply the first equation by 2 and the second equation by 3: $6a + 4p = 1260$ $6a + 9p = 1860$

Next, subtract one equation from the other to eliminate the a terms. $9p − 4p = 5p$ and $1860 − 1260 = 600$ so $5p = 600$, which gives $p = 600 ÷ 5 = 120$. Looking back to what p represents: one pear has a mass of 120 g.

Next, replace the value for the mass of a pear in the first equation to find the mass of the apples: $3a + 240 = 630$ so $3a = 630 − 240 = 390$, which gives $a = 390 ÷ 3 = 130$. This means that one apple has a mass of 130 g.

8 130 g

9 120 g (As a check, from the question: the difference between the mass of an apple and the mass of one pear is 10 g. 130 g − 120 g = 10 g (correct))

10 d (120 gingerbread people divided by 3 gives a third that have a white iced mouth; 120 ÷ 3 = 40)

11 b (120 gingerbread people divided by 2 gives a half of the people that have currant eyes and then divided by 5 gives the number that have currant eyes AND a liquorice nose; 120 ÷ 2 ÷ 5 = 12)

12 a (120 gingerbread people divided by 2 then divided by 3 then divided by 5 gives the number of gingerbread people that have currant eyes AND a white iced mouth AND a liquorice nose; 120 ÷ 2 ÷ 3 ÷ 5 = 4)

Test 4

(pages 10–11)

1 c (The only month when the amount of money rises steeply over one month is August)

2 d (The only month when the amount of money falls steeply is October)

3 d (From the graph, Alfie withdrew £100; his dad gave him £80; £100 + £80 = £180 which is 90% of full price; 10% = £180 ÷ 9 = £20, so the full price is £200)

4 17p (£13.60 ÷ 80 cakes = 17p so Evie needs to sell the cakes at 17p to recoup her costs)

5 £18.40 (40p × 80 cakes = £32; £32 − £13.60 = £18.40 so Evie makes £18.40 profit)

6 20% (Evie sells 16 out of 80 cakes. 80 ÷ 16 = 5; this means that $\frac{1}{5}$ of the cakes are sold to one person and $\frac{1}{5}$ is 20%. To check, find 10% (80 ÷ 10 = 8) and double to find 20% (8 × 2 = 16))

7 b (As group B is playing every 5 seconds and group A is playing every 2 seconds, they play together every 10 seconds. Divide the total performance time of 180 seconds by 10 seconds to find the number of times that both groups play together after the start, 18 times, then add on one for the beat at the start of the sequence = 19)

8 c (As group C is playing every 7 seconds and group A is playing every 2 seconds, they will play together every 14 seconds. Divide the total performance time of 180 seconds by 14 seconds to find the time that both groups play together after the start, 12.86 times (rounds down to 12, as we add whole beats only), then add on one for the beat at the start of the sequence = 13)

9 a (As groups A, B and C are all playing together every 70 seconds (2 × 5 × 7), divide the total performance time of 180 seconds by 70 seconds to find how many times they all play together, 2.57 times (rounds down to 2 times), then add on one for the beat at the start of the sequence = 3)

10 c (Groups A, B and C are all playing together every 70 seconds. Divide the performance time of 300 seconds (5 × 60 seconds = 300 seconds) by 70 to find how many times they all play together, 4.29 (rounds down to 4 times), then add on one for the beat at the start of the sequence = 5)

Test 5

(pages 12–13)

1–3 20% of 180 children = 36 children (10% = 18 so 20% = 36) so 36 children have red hair. 180 children − 36 children = 144 children. The ratio between fair hair and dark hair is 1 : 2 so there are 3 parts; 144 ÷ 3 = 48 so 48 children have fair hair and 96 children (2 × 48) have dark hair.

1 e

2 b

3 d

4–5 See chart below. Start by listing numbers that can be quartered with whole number answers, i.e. multiples of 4.

First number	4	8	12	16	20	24	28	32
When quartered	1	2	3	4	5	6	7	8
Added together	5	10	15	20	25	30	35	40
Multiplied together	4	16	36	64	100	144	196	256

4 Look for square numbers, which are in bold.

Example: 20 and 5 (20 + 5 = 25 and 20 × 5 = 100); 25 and 100 are both square numbers which seems to prove Dara's trick.

5 Example: 16 and 4 (16 + 4 = 20 and 16 × 4 = 64); 64 is a square number but 20 is not which disproves Dara's trick.

6 **c** (To find the median, write the heights in order and choose the middle value: 12 13 17 20 25 28 32; 20 cm is the middle value)

7 **b** (To find the mean height of the books, add up the heights and then divide by the number of books; 17 + 13 + 28 + 20 + 32 + 12 + 25 = 147 cm; 147 cm ÷ 7 = 21 cm)

8 **a** (To find the range, subtract the shortest height from the tallest height; 32 cm − 12 cm = 20 cm)

9 105 cm² (The area of each triangle is (5 cm × 7 cm) ÷ 2; there are six of these triangles, so the area of the bottom panel = 6 × (5 cm × 7 cm) ÷ 2 = 105 cm²)

10 320 cm³ (The volume is 10 cm × 8 cm × 4 cm = 320 cm³)

11 £5.67 (Beth needs 15 ml of black paint + 30 ml of gold paint = 45 ml of paint. If it costs 63p for every 5 ml and 45 ml ÷ 5 ml = 9 the paint costs her 9 × 63p = £5.67)

12 18 seconds (The drone takes 3 s to fly 2 m; 12 m ÷ 2 m = 6 so the drone will take 6 times longer to fly 12 m; 3 s × 6 = 18 s)

Test 6

(pages 14–15)

1 **c** (10% of 35 is 3.5, so 20% is 7 miles)

2 **d** (Total distance = 35 miles + 40 miles = 75 miles; she has driven 50 miles; $\frac{50}{75} = \frac{2}{3}$)

3 4 m (The area of a rectangle is $L \times W$ = 48 m²; 48 m² ÷ 12 m = 4 m)

4 96 m³ (The volume of a cuboid is $L \times W \times D$ = 12 m × 4 m × 2 m = 96 m³)

5 64 plants (The perimeter of the pond = 12 m + 12 m + 4 m + 4 m = 32 m. Each plant is 0.5 m apart so 32 m ÷ 0.5 = 64 plants)

6 **d** (If 82 rupees are worth £1 then 82 × 100 = 8200 rupees)

7 **c** (246 dollars ÷ 1.23 = £200)

8 **c** (200 ÷ 1.12 = £178.57)

9–11 Add up the parts of the ratio 2 + 3 + 6 = 11; then divide 11 into 143 seeds to find 13. Finally, multiply each of the parts by 13 to find out how many seeds each girl has.

9 **b** (13 × 2 = 26 seeds)

10 **c** (13 × 3 = 39 seeds)

11 **d** (13 × 6 = 78 seeds)

Test 7

(pages 16–17)

1 £10.02 (Two games cost £24.99 × 2 = £49.98; £60 − £49.98 = £10.02 change)

2 £63.72 (Three games cost £24.99 × 3 = £74.97; Harry bought three games so he receives 15% off. 10% of £74.97 = £7.497; 5% of £74.97 is half of 10% = £3.7485 so 15% = £11.2455; £74.97 − £11.2455 = £63.7245 which rounds to £63.72)

3 £19.99 (Mr Hoskins pays for only 8 games as he gets 2 games free. 8 × £24.99 = £199.92 so the cost per grandchild is £199.92 ÷ 10 = £19.992 which rounds to £19.99)

4 **d** (3 eggs make 12 cakes, 36 ÷ 12 = 3 so she uses 3 times as many eggs to make 36 cakes; 3 eggs × 3 = 9 eggs)

5 **c** (175 g flour makes 12 cakes, 72 ÷ 12 = 6 so she uses 6 times as much flour to make 72 cakes; 175 g × 6 = 1050 g of flour)

6 **c** (150 g sugar makes 12 cakes; 150 ÷ 3 × 2 = 100 g so she can make 12 cakes ÷ 3 × 2 = 8 cakes)

7 Hashmee (Hashmee: 96 pages ÷ 3 = 32 so $\frac{1}{3}$ of the book is 32 pages. Henry: 25% is a quarter so he has read 96 pages ÷ 4 = 24 pages. Harry: 96 pages − 65 pages left = 31 pages read)

8 29 (To find the mean number of pages read by the children, add up the number of pages and then divide by the number of children; 32 + 24 + 31 = 87; 87 ÷ 3 = 29)

9 **d** (If 15 pupils made up 30% of the year group, then 15 ÷ 3 gives 10% of the year group; multiplying this by ten gives 100% of the year group; 15 ÷ 3 × 10 = 50 pupils)

10 d (If 24 pupils made up 40% of the year group, then 24 ÷ 4 gives 10% of the year group; multiplying this by ten gives 100% of the year group; 24 ÷ 4 × 10 = 60 pupils)

11 e (If 20 pupils made up 25% of the year group, then 20 × 4 gives 100% of the year group; 20 × 4 = 80 pupils)

12 d (If 18 pupils made up 15% of the year group, then 18 ÷ 3 gives 5% of the year group; multiplying this by 2 gives 10% then multiplying by 10 again gives 100% of the year group; 18 ÷ 3 × 2 × 10 = 120 pupils)

Test 8

(pages 18–19)

1 160 children (If 40 children = 25% then 100% = 40 children × 4 = 160 children)

2 48 children (160 children = 100% so 10% is 16 children. 30% is 16 children × 3 = 48 children)

3 16 children (10% is 16 children, so 20% is 16 children × 2 = 32 children; 48 − 32 = 16 children)

4–5 1 cm on the map is equivalent to 250 000 cm in reality. Dividing 250 000 cm by 100 then by 1000 gives how many kilometres are represented by 1 cm. 250 000 cm = 2500 m = 2.5 km. Every 1 cm on the map represents 2.5 km in reality.

4 17.5 km (If 1 cm is equivalent to 2.5 km, then 7 cm is equivalent to 17.5 km (7 × 2.5 km = 17.5 km))

5 9.6 cm (If 2.5 km is equivalent to 1 cm, then 24 km is equivalent to 9.6 cm (24 km ÷ 2.5 km = 9.6))

6 a $(n - 8)$

7 b $(m + 13)$

8 c $(m + n + p) ÷ 3$

9–12 Add up the parts in the ratio to find the total number of parts; 1 + 2 + 3 + 4 = 10. Then divide 10 into 2500 books to find the value of one part; 2500 ÷ 10 = 250. Finally, multiply 250 by each of the parts in the ratio.

9 250 books (Year 3 have 250 × 1 = 250 books)

10 300 books (Year 4 have 250 × 2 = 500 books; 60% are paperback; 10% = 500 ÷ 10 = 50; 60% = 50 × 6 = 300)

11 525 books (Year 5 have 250 × 3 = 750 books; 70% are fiction; 10% = 750 ÷ 10 = 75; 70% = 75 × 7 = 525)

12 120 books (Year 6 have 250 × 4 = 1000 books; 40% are hardback; 10% = 1000 ÷ 10 = 100; 40% = 100 × 4 = 400; 30% of these are factual; 10% of 400 = 40; 30% = 40 × 3 = 120)

Test 9

(pages 20–21)

1–2 Work out how much a kilogram of flour costs for each size of bag. 5 kg bag costs £3.40 so 1 kg costs £3.40 ÷ 5 = 68p

1 kg bag costs £1.80

750 g bag costs £1.40 so 1 kg costs £1.40 ÷ 3 × 4 = £1.87 (rounded)

500 g bag costs 95p so 1 kg costs 95p × 2 = £1.90

1 5 kg bag costs the least per kilogram (68p)

2 500 g bag costs the most per kilogram (£1.90)

3 b (115 − 65 = 50)

4 b $(\frac{100}{500} = 20\%)$

5 e $(\frac{140}{500} = \frac{7}{25})$

6 89 (The first number plus the second number makes the third number, the second number plus the third number makes the fourth number, and so on; 1 + 2 = 3, 2 + 3 = 5, etc.)

7 56 (The difference increases by one each time; +0, +1, +2, +3, +4, etc.)

8 42 (Alternating multiples of 6 with multiples of 7; 6, 7, 12, 14, 18, 21, 24, 28, 30, 35, 36, 42, **42**)

9–10 To make the m term the same in both equations, multiply the first equation by 4 and the second equation by 3:

12m + 16b = 4000 g and 12m + 15b = 3840 g

Next, subtract one equation from the other to eliminate the m terms. This gives b = 160 g.

Next, replace the mass of each metal block b in the first equation to find the mass of the magnets: 3m + (4 × 160 g) = 1000 g; 4 × 160 g = 640 g so take this from 1000 g to find the mass of three magnets; 1000 g − 640 g = 360 g. 3m = 360 g so each magnet has a mass of 360 g ÷ 3 = 120 g.

9 a

10 c

Test 10

(pages 22–23)

1 20% ($\frac{30}{150} = \frac{10}{50} = \frac{1}{5}$ = 20%)

2 $\frac{3}{10}$ ($\frac{45}{150} = \frac{9}{30} = \frac{3}{10}$)

3 c (Mo buys 33 cases (£20 ÷ 60p = 33.33 which rounds to 33. If Mo sells the 33 cases for £1 each he will have 33 × £1 = £33. He needs to take off the £20 that he spent in buying the cases (£33 – £20 = £13). Mo will have a maximum profit of £13.

4 d (120 phone cases cost him 120 × 60p = £72 so £72 cost price is covered when Mo sells 72 cases)

5 d (200 phone cases cost him 200 × 60p = £120; 200 cases ÷ 4 = 50 sets. He sells these for £3 each so takes £150. The maximum profit Mo can make selling the cases in sets of four is £150 – £120 = £30)

6–8 The scale means that 1 cm on the map represents 640 000 cm in reality. This is the same as 1 cm representing 6400 m or 1 cm representing 6.4 km.

6 0.25 cm (If 6.4 km is represented by 1 cm on the map, then 1.6 km is represented by 0.25 cm on the map (1.6 ÷ 6.4 = 0.25))

7 153.6 km (If 1 cm is equivalent to 6.4 km, then 24 cm is equivalent to 153.6 km (6.4 km × 24 = 153.6 km))

8 675 km (If 450 km is $\frac{2}{3}$, divide by 2 then multiply by 3 to find 100% of the journey; 450 ÷ 2 = 225; 225 × 3 = 675 km)

9 c (To find the mean of the scores, add up the scores and then divide by the number of scores; 17 + 18 + 20 + 16 + 19 = 90; 90 ÷ 5 = 18)

10 b (To find the median, order the scores: 16, 17, **18**, 19, 20 then select the middle score of 18, which is Fred)

11 d (The range is the largest score minus the smallest score; 20 – 16 = 4)

Test 11

(pages 24–25)

1 Thursday (There were the least sales on Thursday)

2 Saturday (There were the most sales on Saturday)

3 71 (12 + 10 + 10 + 3 + 8 + 14 + 14 = 71 cups of tea)

4–6 Divide 184 pupils plus 8 teachers (192 people) by 56 people that each coach can carry; 192 ÷ 56 = 3.428; this must be rounded up to a whole number of coaches so no people are left behind, making 4 coaches in total. Each coach costs £175; £175 × 4 = £700; museum entry for 192 people = 192 × £1.75 = £336; total costs = £700 + £336 = £1036

4 4

5 £1036

6 £5.40 (£1036 ÷ 192 = £5.40 each when rounded to the nearest pence)

7 a (Each table and its chairs need an area of 2 m × 2 m and we need a walkway of 2 m in each direction. We can place 5 tables across and 5 tables down. 5 × 5 tables is a total of 25 tables)

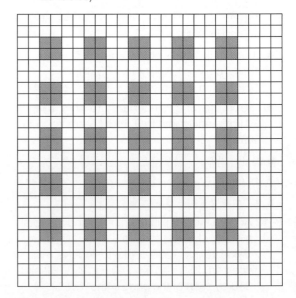

8 c (Each table and its chairs need an area of 2 m × 2 m and we need a walkway of 2 m in each direction. We can place 5 tables down, but as we have an extra 6 metres width, we

can fit 7 tables across. 5 × 7 tables is a total of 35 tables)

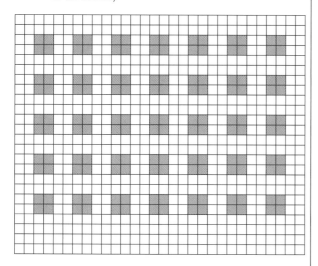

Test 12

(pages 26–27)

1–3 For one model Jas needs 1 head, 1 body, 3 eyes and 5 legs.

Jas can only make as many models as the maximum number of items that he needs divided into the number of items he has.

1 4 models (Jas has 20 each of head, body, eyes and legs; 20 legs ÷ 5 legs per model = 4 models)

2 6 models (Jas has 31 legs so 31 legs ÷ 5 legs per model = 6 r 1 so 6 whole models)

3 16 heads, 16 bodies, 48 eyes, 80 legs (Multiply each part in the ratio by 16)

4–6 A probability outcomes table is the best way of working these options out. If Alice has two 1–6 dice, these are the options she can score:

	1	2	3	4	5	6
1	2	3	4	5	6	7
2	3	4	5	6	7	8
3	4	5	6	7	8	9
4	5	6	7	8	9	10
5	6	7	8	9	10	11
6	7	8	9	10	11	12

4 a (30 single-digit outcomes ÷ 36 total outcomes = $\frac{30}{36} = \frac{5}{6}$)

5 d (15 prime number outcomes ÷ 36 total outcomes = $\frac{15}{36} = \frac{5}{12}$)

6 e (7 square number outcomes ÷ 36 total outcomes = $\frac{7}{36}$)

7 d (If she takes 6 minutes to walk $\frac{3}{5}$ of the way then $\frac{1}{5}$ of the way takes 6 minutes ÷ 3 = 2 minutes; so the whole walk takes 2 minutes × 5 = 10 minutes)

8 b (5 km per hour = 5000 m in 60 minutes so she walks 5000 m ÷ 60 minutes = 83.3 metres per minute; 83.3 metres per minute × 10 minutes = 833 m)

9 e (Beth walks for 10 minutes a day each way, which is 10 × 2 = 20 minutes per day and 20 × 6 = 120 minutes at the end of 6 days. There are 60 minutes in 1 hour, so 120 minutes = 2 hours. Beth walks 5 kilometres per hour so in 2 hours she walks 10 kilometres. Alternatively, Beth walks from home to the library 6 times, and back from the library to home 6 times, so multiply the answer to Q8 by 12 (833 m × 12 = 9996 m), divide by 1000 to convert to kilometres (9.996 km), then round to the nearest kilometre (10 km))

10 e (There are 64 packs × 25 boxes × 2 pallets = 3200 packs of soap)

11 b (£1024 costs ÷ £2.50 per pack = 409.60 so Jet needs to sell 410 packs of soap before he makes a profit)

12 d (If Jet sells all 3200 packs of soap for £2.50, he makes £3200 × £2.50 = £8000. However, he must subtract the cost of the soap, which is £1024. This leaves him with a maximum profit of £6976)

13 b (Divide 3200 packs of soap by 3 to find out how many sets of three Jet can sell: 3200 ÷ 3 = 1066.67, which is 1066 whole sets. Selling these 1066 sets of soap at £5 each = 1066 × £5 = £5330. Finally, take away the cost of the soap to find the maximum profit Jet can make; £5330 − £1024 = £4306)

Test 13

(pages 28–29)

1 13:50 (The 13:50 bus from the station will get to the shops for 14:08)

2 14:23 (The 464 bus gets to the market at 13:58. The next bus to stop at the market gets to the shops at 14:23)

3 10 minutes (14:13 – 14:23)

4–6 The three children start with 60 stickers each (180 ÷ 3 = 60).

4 **d** (Michael gives away $\frac{1}{4}$ (60 – 15 = 45). He gains 12 so has 57)

5 **d** (Brooke gives away 30% (60 – 18 = 42). She gains 15 so has 57)

6 **b** (Stanley gives away 20% (60 – 12 = 48). He gains 18 so has 66)

7 £172 000 (4 rounds down)

8 £172 500 (9 rounds up)

9 £170 000 (2 rounds down)

10 £200 000 (7 rounds up)

11 7 and 12 (7 + 12 = 19, 7 × 12 = 84)

12 4 and 11 (4 + 11 = 15, 4 × 11 = 44)

13 3 and 13 (3 + 13 = 16, 3 × 13 = 39)

14 5 and 6 (5 + 6 = 11, 5 × 6 = 30)

Test 14

(pages 30–31)

1 48 °C (Difference = 39 – −9 = 39 + 9 = 48)

2 33 °C (39 + 32 + 28 = 99; 99 ÷ 3 = 33)

3 −2 °C (−9 + −2 + 5 = −6; −6 ÷ 3 = −2)

4 41 °C (Difference = 32 – −9 = 32 + 9 = 41; Baghdad is 32 degrees warmer than 0 °C and Anchorage is 9 degrees below 0 °C, which is a total of 41 degrees different)

5 80p (2 days × 10p per day = 20p for each book; 20p × 4 = 80p)

6 70p (7 days × 10p per day = 70p)

7 £5.80 (14 days × 10p per day = £1.40 for each book; £1.40 × 3 = £4.20; her change is £10 – £4.20 = £5.80)

8 **c** (2 shirts at £25 each = 2 × £25 = £50; 10% of £50 is £5 so 30% of £50 is £15; £50 – £15 = £35)

9 **d** (£50 – £32.50 = £17.50; £17.50 ÷ £50 = £35 ÷ £100 = 35%)

10 1258 cm² (The area of the sail is (38 cm × 18 cm) ÷ 2 = 342 cm². The area of the material is 40 cm × 40 cm = 1600 cm². The total amount of material left over is 1600 cm² – 342 cm² = 1258 cm²)

11 5 holes (18 cm is the same as 180 mm. 180 mm ÷ 36 mm = 5 holes)

12 75 mm or 7.5 cm (37.5 cm is the same as 375 mm. 375 mm ÷ 5 holes = 75 mm of thread)

Test 15

(pages 32–33)

1 33 (Programme 2: (3 + 8) × 3 = 33)

2 68 (Programme 3: 12 × 4 + 20 = 68)

3 57 (Programme 1: 15 × 3 + 12 = 57)

4 18:08 (5:56 p.m. + 12 min = 6:08 p.m. which is 18:08 in 24-hour time)

5 18:11 (Add 3 minutes because Philip's watch is fast)

6 18:39 (On Philip's watch, he gets home at 18:11 + 20 min + 8 min = 18:39)

7–8 The map scale means that 1 cm on the map represents 45 000 cm in reality. Dividing 45 000 cm by 100 (to make 450 metres) then by 1000 (to make 0.45 km) makes it easier to solve these problems. 1 cm is equivalent to 0.45 km.

7 2.25 km (If 1 cm is equivalent to 0.45 km, then 5 cm is equivalent to 2.25 km (0.45 km × 5 = 2.25 km))

8 13.33 cm (If 0.45 km is represented by 1 cm, then 6 km is represented by 13.33 cm (6 km ÷ 0.45 km = 13.33 cm))

9 **c** (To find the mean height of the rabbits, add up the heights and then divide by the number of rabbits; 35 cm ÷ 5 = 7 cm)

10 **d** (To find the mean mass of the rabbits, add up the masses and then divide by the number of rabbits; 405 g ÷ 5 = 81 g)

11 **b** (To find the range of the masses, subtract the lowest mass from the highest mass; 110 g – 45 g = 65 g)

12 **c** (To find the range of the heights, subtract the shortest height from the tallest height; 9 cm – 5 cm = 4 cm)

Test 16

(pages 34–35)

1 **e** (Adding 10% of the outstanding amount each day that the money is owing gives, 4th Dec: £20 + £2 = £22; 5th Dec: £22 + £2.20 = £24.20; 6th Dec: £24.20 + £2.42 = £26.62)

2 d (Adding 10% of the outstanding amount each day that the money is owing gives, Sun: £10 + £1 = £11; Mon: £11 + £1.10 = £12.10; Tue: £12.10 + £1.21 = £13.31)

3 c (£9.68 ÷ 110 × 100 = £8.80; £8.80 ÷ 110 × 100 = £8)

4 c (720 ÷ 5 × 3 = 432)

5 b (720 − 432 = 288; 288 ÷ 2 evenings = 144 pieces per night)

6 c (144 pieces ÷ 2.5 = 57.6, or 288 ÷ 5 = 57.6, which rounds up to 58)

7 1.85 m^2 ((0.75 m × 0.6 m × 2) + (0.6 m × 0.35 m × 2) + (0.75 m × 0.35 m × 2) = 0.9 m + 0.42 m + 0.525 m = 1.845 m; this rounds to 1.85 m^2. Also accept 18 450 cm^2)

8 Yes, Merry does have enough paper. Merry has paper that is 300 cm × 100 cm. Working out the overall area is not helpful as the paper has to fit the shape of the box. The quick way of solving this is to round up each measurement to the nearest 50 cm. That gives us measurements of 100 cm × 50 cm × 100 cm. We can fit 3 × 100 cm across the length of the paper and 1 × 100 cm along the width of the paper so yes, Merry does have enough paper.

9 0.1575 m^3 (To find the volume, multiply the three dimensions together (75 cm × 60 cm × 35 cm = 157 500 cm^3) and then convert to m^3 by dividing by 1 000 000 (157 500 ÷ 1 000 000 = 0.1575 m^3). Alternatively, convert the measurement into metres first and then multiply (0.75 × 0.6 × 0.35 = 0.1575 m^3))

10 £32 (Add up the £10, £8 and £14)

11 £27.20 (10% of £32 is £3.20. Halve this to find 5%. Add the two values together to make 15%; £3.20 + £1.60 = £4.80; cost after discount = £32 − £4.80 = £27.20)

12 £12.80 (£40 − £27.20 = £12.80)

Test 17

(pages 36–37)

1 e (The highest point of the graph is 18 km)

2 b (The flat part of the graph at 18 km is from 10:30 to 11:30 which is 1 hour)

3 d (The distance does not change from 13:00 to 13:30)

4 d (Austin has 70 counters altogether. $\frac{14}{70} = \frac{7}{35} = \frac{1}{5} = \frac{2}{10} = 20\%$)

5 c (27 + 12 = 39 so probability of white or blue = $\frac{39}{70}$)

6 £22 (£12 + £10 = £22 with the £5 book free)

7 £20.25 (Total cost = £27; 25% is $\frac{1}{4}$ so $\frac{1}{4}$ of £27 is £6.75; £27 − £6.75 = £20.25)

8 £19.75 (£40 − £20.25 = £19.75)

9–12 Begin with the four shapes that are the same. The four dark grey boxes have a total mass of 344 g so dividing this by four gives the mass of one box: 344 ÷ 4 = 86 g. Next, solve the top-left set by taking 86 g from 737 g and then dividing the answer by three to find mass of the pale grey cylinders: 737 g − 86 g = 651 g; 651 g ÷ 3 = 217 g. Next, use the same process for solving the bottom-left set to find the mass of the white cylinders: 447 g − 86 g − 217 g = 144 g; 144 g ÷ 2 = 72 g. Finally, solve the top-right set to find the mass of the dark grey cylinders: 450 g − 72 g − 72 g = 306 g. 306 g ÷ 2 = 153 g.

9 217 g

10 86 g

11 72 g

12 153 g

13 132 g (To find the mean, add up the four masses and then divide the answer by four: 528 ÷ 4 = 132 g)

Test 18

(pages 38, 59)

1 66 m^2 ((15 m × 4 m) + (3 m × 4 m ÷ 2) = 60 m^2 + 6 m^2 = 66 m^2)

2 10 times larger (60 m^2 ÷ 6 m^2 = 10)

3 £231.12 (The cost of the stones is £263.90 (145 × £1.82). There is a 20% discount to subtract (10% of £263.90 is £26.39, so 20% is £26.39 × 2 = £52.78). After the discount the cost is therefore £263.90 − £52.78 = £211.12. Mrs Basley doesn't spend over £275 so she has to add on £20 for delivery. £211.12 + £20 = £231.12)

4 c (To find the mean mass of the dogs, add up the masses and then divide by the number of dogs; 32 kg + 60 kg + 16 kg + 48 kg + 4 kg = 160 kg; 160 kg ÷ 5 = 32 kg)

5 a (Twinkle's mass is the middle value)

6–8 Begin with the known number: 13 toffees. Then express $\frac{2}{5}$ as a percentage; $\frac{2}{5}$ = 40%. Next, add together the percentages; 25% + 30% + 40% = 95% so the 13 toffees are 5% of the total number of sweets.

10% of the sweets = 13 × 2 = 26; total number of sweets = 100% of the sweets = 26 × 10 = 260

6 65 sweets are fizzy fruits (260 sweets ÷ 100 × 25 = 65; OR: 25% = 5 × 5% so 25% of the sweets = 5 × 13 = 65)

7 104 sweets are candy canes (260 sweets ÷ 100 × 40 = 104; OR: 40% = 8 × 5% so 40% of the sweets = 8 × 13 = 104)

8 78 sweets are mints (260 sweets ÷ 100 × 30 = 78; OR: 30% = 6 × 5% so 30% of the sweets = 6 × 13 = 78)

9 d (Danni has 84 balls of black wool ÷ 3 balls = 28. Danni needs 3 balls to make 10 sheep so 28 × 10 = 280 sheep)

10 b (Danni needs 5 balls of brown wool to make 10 dogs so $2\frac{1}{2}$ balls of brown wool would make 5 dogs. 25 dogs ÷ 5 dogs = 5 so she needs 5 × $2\frac{1}{2}$ = $12\frac{1}{2}$ balls of brown wool)

11 a (Danni needs $\frac{1}{4}$ of a ball of black wool to make 10 polar bears so to make 40 polar bears she needs $\frac{1}{4}$ × 4 = 1 ball of black wool)

12 d (Danni needs 8 balls of white wool to make 10 polar bears. She has 50 balls of white wool, 50 ÷ 8 = 6.25; multiply this by 10 as each proportion makes 10 polar bears; 6.25 × 10 = 62.5 polar bears which rounds down to 62 as she cannot make half a polar bear)

Test 19

(pages 60–61)

1 No, Michael is incorrect because in Year 6 the boys read more books than the girls.

2 Yes, Jodie is correct because there are more books read in Years 5 and 6 (60 books) than in Years 3 and 4 (47 books).

3 4.5 (Year 3 = (10 + 12) ÷ 2 = 11; Year 4 = (12 + 13) ÷ 2 = 12.5; Year 5 = (14 + 15) ÷ 2 = 14.5; Year 6 = (16 + 15) ÷ 2 = 15.5; 15.5 − 11 = 4.5)

4 d (In the formula $2p + 8 = s$ replace p with 12 guests; (2 × 12) + 8 = size of cake; 24 + 8 = 32 cm³)

5 c (In the formula $2p + 8 = s$ replace p with 85 guests; (2 × 85) + 8 = size of cake; 170 + 8 = 178 cm³)

6 d (In the formula $2p + 8 = s$ replace s with 420 cm³; (2 × p) + 8 = 420; 420 − 8 = 412; 412 ÷ 2 = 206 guests)

7 64 (The cube numbers with two digits are 27 and 64; 64 is the number that is also a square)

8 368 and 360 (First divide the number in two: 728 ÷ 2 = 364; then, to make a difference of 8, add 4 to one number and subtract 4 from the other: 364 + 4 = 368; 364 − 4 = 360)

9 92 (13 × 3 = 39; 39 + 7 = 46; 46 × 2 = 92)

10 140 (21 × 3 = 63; 63 + 7 = 70; 70 × 2 = 140)

11 218 (34 × 3 = 102; 102 + 7 = 109; 109 × 2 = 218)

Test 20

(pages 62–63)

1 e (Ingredients are for 50 cheese sticks so she needs to increase the butter in proportion to make 175 cheese sticks. 50 cheese sticks ÷ 2 = 25 sticks. 175 ÷ 25 = 7 so she needs 150 g ÷ 2 × 7 = 525 g butter)

2 a (200 g of cheese makes 50 cheese sticks, but Mrs Cherry only has 40 g. 200 g ÷ 40 g = 5, so she can only make $\frac{1}{5}$ of 50 cheese sticks. $\frac{1}{5}$ of 50 = 10 cheese sticks)

3 70 000 cm³ (Volume = 40 cm × 35 cm × 50 cm = 70 000 cm³)

4 10 300 cm² (Surface area = (40 cm × 35 cm × 2) + (40 cm × 50 cm × 2) + (35 cm × 50 cm × 2) = 10 300 cm²)

5 Yes, Juliet does have enough paper. (Juliet has paper that is 200 cm × 150 cm. Working out the area is not helpful as the paper has to fit the shape of the box. The quick way of solving this is to round up each measurement to 50 cm. You can then fit four 50 cm by 50 cm squares along the length and three 50 cm by 50 cm squares along the width, so Juliet does have enough paper)

6 c (658 flyers ÷ 14 roads = 47 houses per road)

7 a (120 flyers in 60 minutes = 2 flyers per minute)

8 b (658 flyers ÷ 2 flyers per minute = 329 minutes or 5h 29min)

9 c (Yanick is paid £1 (1p × 100) for the first 100 flyers, £2 (2p × 100) for the second 100, £3 (3p × 100) for the third 100, £4 (4p × 100) for the fourth 100, £5 (5p × 100) for the fifth 100 and £6 (6p × 100) for the sixth 100; £1 + £2 + £3 + £4 + £5 + £6 = £21. He is paid 7p per flyer for the remaining 58 flyers (7p × 58 = £4.06). £21 + £4.06 = £25.06)

10 30000 (20 pencils × 125 boxes × 12 cartons × 1 pallet = 30000 pencils)

11 3334 (£900 ÷ 27p = 90000 ÷ 27 = 3333.3 recurring, so 3334 pencils need to be sold to break even)

12 £7200 (30000 × 27p = £8100; £8100 − £900 = £7200)

13 £6900 (15000 × 27p = £4050; 15000 × 25p = £3750; £4050 + £3750 = £7800; £7800 − £900 = £6900)

Test 21

(pages 64–65)

1–2 For every 66ml of paint, Rosalind needs to add 33ml × 5 of water. This gives 66ml + 165ml = 231ml of mixed paint.

Every tube of paint is 33ml. A ratio table like this can be helpful in questions like these.

1 495ml of water (6 × 33ml = 198ml of paint; 198 is 2 parts; the water is 5 parts; 198 ÷ 2 × 5 = 495ml of water)

2 400ml of paint (1 litre of water is 5 parts; 1 part = 1000ml ÷ 5 = 200ml; the paint is 2 parts; 200ml × 2 = 400ml)

3 c (The 'Dairy' sector is less than half of the size of the 'Meat, fish and vegetarian alternatives' sector so we know that the answer cannot be **d** or **e**. The 'Dairy' sector is not as small as a quarter of the 'Meat, fish and vegetarian alternatives' sector so we know the answer cannot be **a** or **b**. The sector is a little smaller than half of the 'Meat, fish and vegetarian alternatives' sector so we know that **c** is the correct answer)

4 d (The 'Vegetables, salad and fruit' sector is slightly less than half of the pie chart (50%) and more than a third (33%) so it must be 45%)

5 c (The 'Meat, fish and vegetarian alternatives' sector is a quarter of the pie chart = 90°)

6 £21.85 (three cake tins = £18; icing kit = £5; £18 + £5 = £23; 5% off when you spend £20; 10% is £2.30, so 5% is £1.15; £23 − £1.15 = £21.85)

7 £54.40 (four towels = £32, travel case = £36, £32 + £36 = £68; 20% off when you spend £60; 10% is £6.80, so 20% is £13.60; £68 − £13.60 = £54.40)

8 £13.20 (one kettle at £24 + one toaster at £28 = £52; 10% off when you spend £40; £52 − £5.20 = £46.80; £60 − £46.80 = £13.20 change)

Number of parts (tubes) of paint	Amount of paint in ml	Number of parts of water	Amount of water in ml	Number of parts of mixed paint	Amount of mixed paint in ml
2	66	5	165	7	231
4	132	10	330	14	462
6	198	15	495	21	693
8	264	20	660	28	924
10	330	25	825	35	1155

9–10 Multiply the first equation by 3 then subtract the second equation to eliminate c: $15c + 9b = £9.75$; $15c + 1b = £4.55$

$8b = £9.75 - £4.55 = £5.20$ so price of each book $b = £5.20 ÷ 8 = 65p$

Next, replace the cost of the book in the second equation to find the cost of a crayon, c: $15c + 65p = £4.55$

Finally, subtract 65p from each side: $15c = £3.90$ so one crayon costs $£3.90 ÷ 15 = 26p$)

9 65p

10 26p

11–13 To solve this type of question it is easiest to begin with what you know. Sushi is about to start nursery, so she must be 1, 2, 3 or 4. Ben is 3 years older than Sushi, so he must be 4, 5, 6 or 7. Reuben is 5 years older than Ben, so he must be 9, 10, 11 or 12. Reuben is $\frac{1}{4}$ of his mother's age, so multiply his possible ages by 4 to find out his mother's possible ages: 36, 40, 44 or 48. The father is 5 years older than the mother, so he must be 41, 45, 49 or 53.

Ben is $\frac{1}{9}$ of his father's age, so multiply Ben's possible ages (4, 5, 6, 7) by 9 and see if the answers match his father's possible ages (41, 45, 49, 53). $4 × 9 = 36$ (not a match); $5 × 9 = 45$ (a match); $6 × 9 = 54$ (not a match); $7 × 9 = 63$ (not a match). As there is only one match, you now know everyone's age. Their father is 45, their mother is 40, Reuben is 10, Ben is 5 and Sushi is 2.

11 10

12 45

13 2

Test 22

(pages 66–67)

1 b (To find the mean mass of the gem stones, add up the masses and then divide by the number of stones; $28 + 47 + 63 + 15 + 104 + 20 + 83 = 360$; $360 ÷ 7 = 51.43$ g which rounds to 51 g)

2 e (To find the range of the masses, subtract the lightest mass from the heaviest mass; 104 g $– 15$ g $= 89$ g)

3 8 350 000 km (When rounding 8 354 612 km to the nearest ten thousand, you need to look at the value of the number in the thousands column. This is 4 so round down)

4 978 674 729 221 (978 675 642 000 – 912 779 = 978 674 729 221)

5 12 800 000 km (When rounding 12 788 314 km to the nearest hundred thousand, you need to look at the value of the number in the ten thousands column. This is 8 so round up)

6 e (The area of the square car park is 750 m × 750 m = 562 500 m²)

7 d (Each side of the car park is 0.75 km which is the same as 750 m. The width of each car park space is 2.7 m; 750 m ÷ 2.7 m = 277.78 which rounds down to 277 whole car parking spaces in each row. The length of each car parking space is 12.2 m; 750 m ÷ 12.2 m = 61.475 which rounds down to 61 whole car parking spaces in each column. Total number of car parking spaces = 277 × 61 = 16 897)

8 c (16 897 ÷ 100 × 85 = 14 362.45, which rounds to 14 362)

9 b (220 mini monsters ÷ 4 = 55, so 55 mini monsters have a green ribbon in their hair. 55 mini monsters ÷ 5 = 11, so 11 mini monsters have a green ribbon in their hair AND have a silver antenna)

10 a (220 mini monsters ÷ 5 = 44, so 44 mini monsters have a silver antenna. 44 mini monsters ÷ 9 = 4.89; cannot have a part of a monster so this rounds down to 4 monsters having a silver antenna AND a purple curly tail)

11 e (220 mini monsters ÷ 4 = 55, so 55 mini monsters have a green ribbon in their hair. 55 mini monsters ÷ 5 = 11, so 11 mini monsters have a green ribbon in their hair AND have a silver antenna. 11 ÷ 9 = 1.22; cannot have a part of a monster so 1 monster has a green ribbon in its hair AND a silver antenna AND a purple curly tail)

Test 23

(pages 68–69)

1 a (If 57 is $\frac{3}{4}$ of the queue, then $\frac{1}{4}$ of the queue = 57 ÷ 3 = 19; the whole queue = 19 × 4 = 76)

2 d (If 24 minutes = 20% then 100% = 24 × 5 = 120 minutes)

3 b (18:10 – 17:40 = 30 minutes; 120 minutes ÷ 30 minutes = 4; 100 ÷ 4 = 25%)

4 24, 36, 48 (12 × 2 red beads = 24; 12 × 3 white beads = 36 beads; 12 × 4 striped beads = 48)

5 No, Samuel does not have enough beads to make 35 monsters. (35 × 2 red beads = 70; 35 × 3 white beads = 105 beads; 35 × 4 = 140 striped beads. Samuel has enough red beads and white beads, but he does not have enough striped beads)

6 £202.80 (Work out the cost of one monster: (2 × 13p) + (3 × 17p) + (4 × 23p) = 26p + 51p + 92p = £1.69; cost of 120 monsters = 120 × £1.69 = £202.80)

7–8 Start by creating two equations where x = mass of one onion in grams and p = mass of one parsnip in grams.

$5x + p = 680$ and $x + 4p = 440$

Then multiply the first equation by 4 to make the p term the same in both equations.

$(5x + p = 680) × 4 = 20x + 4p = 2720$

Next, subtract one equation from the other to eliminate the p terms.

$20x + 4p = 2720$

$- x + 4p = 440$

so $19x = 2280$

Next, divide by 19 to find the mass of one onion: $x = 2280 ÷ 19 = 120$ (g)

Finally, replace the mass of onions at 120 g each to find the mass of each parsnip:

$(5 × 120) + p = 680$

$600 + p = 680$

$680 – 600 = 80$ so the mass of one parsnip is 80 g

7 c

8 b

9 9 and 3 (9 squared is 81 and 3 cubed is 27)

10 7 and 4 (7 squared is 49 and 4 cubed is 64)

11 8 and 2 (8 squared is 64 and 2 cubed is (0)8)

12 6 and 1 (6 squared is 36 and 1 cubed is (0)1)

Test 24

(pages 70–71)

1–3 Work out the possible numbers first:

Square numbers less than 40 (1, 4, 9, 16, 25, 36)

All of the number must be even (4, 16, 36)

Cube numbers less than 40 (1, 8, 27)

All of the numbers must be even (8)

Now we are looking for the ratio 1 : 2 : 3 so we can look at the following combinations:

4 : 8 : 12 – this is a possible answer as 4 is a square number and 8 is a cube number.

8 : 16 : 24 – this isn't a possible answer as the total comes to 48 and we need a total number of less than 40.

1 4

2 8

3 12

4–5 The scale means that 1 cm on the map represents 80 000 cm in reality. This is the same as 1 cm representing 800 m or 1 cm representing 0.8 km.

4 d (If 1 cm is equivalent to 0.8 km, then 1.6 km is represented by 2 cm on the map (1.6 km ÷ 0.8 km = 2 cm))

5 b (If 1 cm is equivalent to 800 m, then 0.75 cm is equivalent to 600 m (800 m ÷ 4 × 3 = 600 m))

6 e (Rings £9.02 profit; necklaces £3.40 profit; bracelets £7.20 profit; hair clips loss of 73p; brooches £42.33 profit; so brooches made the most profit)

7 b (Necklaces made a 40% profit: £8.50 ÷ 100 × 40 = £3.40)

8 b (£0.73 is one tenth of £7.30, so loss = 10%)

9 2592 (24 packets × 36 boxes × 3 pallets = 2592 packets of batteries)

10 1080 (£648 per pallet × 3 pallets = £1944; Mr Ramsay sells a packet of batteries for £1.80; £1944 ÷ £1.80 = 1080 so Mr Ramsay has to sell 1080 packets of batteries before he is able to make a profit)

11 £2721.60 (If he sells 2592 packets of batteries at £1.80, he gets £4665.60; taking off the cost of £1944, the total profit possible is £2721.60; OR: once he has covered his costs, the money he makes from the remaining batteries is all profit: 2592 – 1080 = 1512; 1512 × £1.80 = £2721.60)

12 £36.72 (24 packets costing £1.80 each = £43.20; discount is 15%; 10% = £4.32, so 5% = £2.16, so total discount = £4.32 + £2.16 = £6.48; customer pays £43.20 – £6.48 = £36.72)

Test 25

(pages 72–73)

1 **c** (Cost of order = 2 × £4.75 + £8.99 + £3.75 = £22.24)

2 **e** (Cost of order = £4.75 + £8.99 + £2.20 + £3.75 = £19.69;

Mr Walker pays with £20 so his change = £20 – £19.69 = 31p)

3 **b** (Cost of order = 2 × (£4.75 + £8.99) + £3.75 = £31.23;

Janice pays with £40 so her change = £40 – £31.23 = £8.77)

4–5 For these questions, a grid is an easy way of tracking movements.

4 **b**

5 **e**

6 13 minutes

7 40 °C

8 11 minutes (20 minutes – 9 minutes = 11 minutes)

Test 26

(pages 74–75)

1 4 and 6 (4 + 6 = 10; 4 × 6 = 24)

2 7 and 8 (7 + 8 = 15; 7 × 8 = 56)

3 9 and 2 (9 + 2 = 11; 9 × 2 = 18)

4 300 cm (350 cm – 50 cm = 300 cm)

5 175 cm (To work out the median, first put the heights in order: 50, 75, 150, **150**, **200**, 300, 300, 350; there are two middle values, so median = (150 cm + 200 cm) ÷ 2 = 175 cm)

6 **c** (If 1 mile = 1.6 km, then 100 miles = 160 km)

7 **a** (68 miles ÷ 100 miles = 68%; 100% – 68% = 32%)

8 **c** (105 minutes ÷ 68 miles = 1.54 minutes per mile; 100 miles × 1.54 minutes per mile = 154 minutes; 12:30 p.m. + 154 minutes = 3:04 p.m.)

9–11 The scale 1 : 720 000 means that 1 cm represents 720 000 cm. This is the same as 1 cm representing 7200 m or 1 cm representing 7.2 km.

9 **b** (If 7.2 km is represented by 1 cm on the map, then 3.6 km is represented by 0.5 cm on the map)

10 **c** (If 1 cm on the map is equivalent to 7.2 km, 0.5 cm on the map is equivalent to 7.2 km ÷ 2 = 3.6 km; so 1.5 cm on the map is equivalent to 7.2 km + 3.6 cm = 10.8 km)

11 **a** (Take the total of 10.8 km, then divide it into thirds = 3.6 km)

12 **c** (If 7.2 km is represented by 1 cm on the map, then 108 km is represented by 108 ÷ 7.2 = 15 cm)

Test 27

(pages 76–77)

1 80 pupils (If 30% of Year 4 = 24 pupils, then 8 pupils = 10% so 100% = 8 pupils × 10 = 80 pupils)

2 45 pupils (If $\frac{3}{5}$ = 27 pupils, then 9 pupils = $\frac{1}{5}$ so the total number of pupils = 9 pupils × 5 = 45 pupils)

3 209 pupils (If $\frac{1}{4}$ of year 6 = 21 pupils, then 21 × 4 = 84 pupils. 80 pupils in Year 4 + 45 pupils in Year 5 + 84 pupils in Year 6 = 209 pupils)

4–6 Garden centre buys 4 fountains × 5 boxes × 6 cartons × 2 pallets = 240 fountains. They pay for 2 pallets at £2700 per pallet = £5400

4 **d** (To cover their costs they must sell £5400 ÷ £75 = 72 fountains)

5 **d** (£75 × 240 fountains = £18 000; total profit = £18 000 – £5400 = £12 600)

6 **c** (Sale price at 10% off = £75 ÷ 100 × 90 = £67.50; total money taken = £75 × 120 fountains + £67.50 × 120 fountains = £9000 + £8100 = £17 100; profit = £17 100 – £5400 = £11 700)

7 **a** (120 stickers ÷ 5 = 24)

8 **b** (120 stickers ÷ 5 = 24; 24 ÷ 4 = 6)

9 **b** (To find the profit, take the 'cost to make' from the 'price sold'; for the Spaceman figure, profit = £30.50 – £8.94 = £21.56)

10 **d** (Profit = price sold for – cost to make; this difference is greatest for the Skater figure)

11 **e** (Multiply the 'cost to make' by 3 to find a selling price with a 200% profit; for the Zombie figure, £7.25 × 3 = £21.75)

Test 28

(pages 78–79)

1 **b** (2 cm × 2 cm × 2 cm = 8 cm³)

2 d ($2\,cm \times 2\,cm \times 6$ faces $= 24\,cm^2$)

3 a ($2 \times 2 \times 2 = 8\,cm^3$; $4 \times 4 \times 4 = 64\,cm^3$;
$\frac{8}{64} = \frac{1}{8}$)

4 d ($64\,cm^3 - 8\,cm^3 = 56\,cm^3$)

5–6 For this scale, 1 cm on the pattern represents 4 cm in reality.

5 16 cm (If 4 cm in reality is represented by 1 cm on the pattern, then 64 cm is represented by 16 cm on the pattern ($64\,cm \div 4 = 16\,cm$))

6 84 cm (If 1 cm on the pattern is equivalent to 4 cm in reality, then 21 cm on the pattern is equivalent to 84 cm in reality ($21\,cm \times 4 = 84\,cm$))

7 6 cm (If 4 cm in reality is represented by 1 cm on the pattern, then 24 cm is represented by 6 cm on the pattern ($24\,cm \div 4 = 6\,cm$))

8 £45.74 (Sam has 3 letters so cost $= £2.25 \times 3 + £38.99 = £45.74$)

9 £7.51 (Betina has 6 letters so cost $= £2.25 \times 6 + £38.99 = £52.49$;

change $= £60 - £52.49 = £7.51$)

10 No (Fitzgerald has 10 letters so cost $= £2.25 \times 10 + £38.99 = £61.49$; OR: 4 more letters than Betina would cost $£2.25 \times 4 = £9$ which is more than the change Betina received)

11 c (To find the mean length of the snails, add up the lengths and divide by the number of snails; $90\,cm \div 5 = 18\,cm$)

12 e (Take away the difference between the length and the height of each snail. Eric has the smallest difference, 9 cm)

13 d (Range = longest length − shortest length $= 20\,cm - 16\,cm = 4\,cm$)

Test 29

(pages 80–81)

1 105.1 m (car and space behind $= 430\,cm + 50\,cm = 480\,cm$; $480\,cm \times 22$ cars $= 10560\,cm$; the 50 cm space **after** the last car is not included in the measurement of cars so length of line $= 10560 - 50 = 10510\,cm$ or 105.1 m)

2 £423 500 (22 cars $\times$ £19 250 $=$ £423 500)

3 2.5 kg

4 160 cm ($42\,kg \div 7$ days $= 6\,kg$ per day)

5 232.5 kg (2 metres corresponds to 7.5 kg food per day; 31 days $\times$ 7.5 kg $= 232.5$ kg)

6 a (It does not matter whether you travel east or north first of all as the result will be the same)

7 c (The vets' lies south-east from the doctors')

8 c (The office lies north-west from the café)

Test 30

(pages 82–83)

1–3 For these questions, start with the 3 grey triangles: $561\,g \div 3 = 187\,g$

Next, look at the 2 black circles and the grey triangle: $657\,g - 187\,g = 470\,g$ so each black circle weighs $470\,g \div 2 = 235\,g$

Next, replace the circle to find the mass of the diamond: $493\,g - 235\,g = 258\,g$; $258\,g \div 2 = 129\,g$

1 129 g

2 235 g

3 187 g

4 c (If I am in 9th place with three others, the four of us take up places 9, 10, 11 and 12; $52 - 12 = 40$)

5 d (Schwartz came 9th, alongside 3 other cars who crossed the finishing line at exactly the same time. So 3 cars came equal to Schwartz and 8 cars did better; $3 + 8 = 11$. There were 52 cars in total, so $\frac{11}{52}$ came equal or better than Schwartz)

6–7 Start by working out the cost of 5 tins at each shop.

Shop 1: £14 $\times$ 5 tins $=$ £70

Shop 2: £16 $\times$ 5 tins $=$ £80; 15% of £80 $=$ £12; £80 − £12 $=$ £68

Shop 3: £20 $\times$ 4 tins $=$ £80 + 1 tin free

6 b

7 e

8 d (Work out the cost of 6 tins at each shop. Shop 1: $6 \times$ £14 $=$ £84; Shop 2: $6 \times$ £16 $=$ £96, taking 15% off gives £96 − £14.40 $=$ £81.60; Shop 3: $2 \times$ (£20 $\times$ 2) $+$ 2 tins free $=$ £80; when there are 2 tins free Shop 3 becomes the cheapest deal)

9 b

10 e

11 b

PUZZLE ANSWERS

Puzzle 1

(page 84)

a $0.6508 + 0.3492 = $ **1**

b $2^2 = $ **4**

c The 4th prime number is **7**

d $2\frac{3}{4} \div \frac{1}{4} = $ **11**

e $50 \times 0.28 = $ **14**

f $39.26 \div 392.6 = $ **10**

g $14\frac{3}{8} + 2\frac{10}{16} = $ **17**

h $4328 \times 0 = $ **0**

The word revealed is 'Hello'.

10	12	8	0	15	9	6	5	3	11	19	14	20	2	6	19	20	16
4	2	13	17	16	5	2	9	15	17	5	7	6	16	9	3	15	12
17	15	5	11	2	3	13	5	2	10	8	17	2	3	2	13	6	2
1	11	14	4	13	1	17	4	16	4	2	1	2	17	17	0	10	11
0	4	10	7	8	10	6	4	2	1	9	4	16	11	16	18	5	10
11	3	9	1	2	0	1	14	13	14	3	7	12	14	9	2	13	4
14	12	2	14	6	7	8	5	6	7	16	10	3	14	15	12	9	7
4	5	8	7	3	11	3	7	12	10	2	4	13	11	3	8	2	14
17	3	6	10	12	14	14	10	5	4	6	4	5	4	11	7	14	10

Puzzle 2

(page 85)

1 384 (There are 32 rows × 8 seats × 2 sides of the aisle. 32 × 8 × 2 = 512 seats. If 512 seats are 100%, then 50% is 512 ÷ 2 = 256; 25% is 256 ÷ 2 = 128; so 75% = 256 + 128 = 384 (OR 75% = 100% − 25%; 512 − 128 = 384)

2 There are **20** red roses, **32** white roses and **20** lilies. (Start with what you know: carnations are 10% of the bouquet and there are 8 of them. If 8 = 10%, then 100% of bouquet = 8 × 10 = 80 flowers.

Red roses are 25%: 80 ÷ 4 = 20

White roses are $\frac{2}{5} = \frac{4}{10}$: 80 ÷ 10 × 4 = 32

Lilies make up the rest: 8 + 20 + 32 = 60 so there are 20 lilies)

3 66 (The first person shakes hands with 11 people. The second person shakes hands with 10 people as they have already shaken hands with the first person. The third person shakes hands with 9 people as they have already shaken hands with the first and second person. This pattern follows so the calculation is 11 + 10 + 9 + 8 + 7 + 6 + 5 + 4 + 3 + 2 + 1 = 66)

4 36 litres of sparkling water (250 ml × 168 glasses = 42 000 ml = 42 litres; the ratio 1 : 6 has 7 parts so one part = 42 litres ÷ 7 = 6 litres; sparkling water is 6 parts of the drink, so need 6 × 6 litres = 36 litres)

5 30 000 cm³ (30 cm × 30 cm × 6 cm = 5400 cm³; 40 cm × 40 cm × 6 cm = 9600 cm³; 50 cm × 50 cm × 6 cm = 15 000 cm³; 5400 cm³ + 9600 cm³ 15 000 cm³ = 30 000 cm³)

Puzzle 3

(page 86)

The ratio of sheep is $3:1:7$ and there is a total of 132 sheep.

The number of parts = $3 + 1 + 7 = 11$ so one part = 132 sheep ÷ 11 = 12 sheep. This means that there are 36, 12 and 84 sheep in Fields 1, 2 and 3.

  1 There are 36 sheep in Field 1.

  2 There are 12 sheep in Field 2.

  3 There are 84 sheep in Field 3.

  4 There are 22 white, male sheep. ($\frac{2}{3}$ of the sheep are white; $132 \div 3 \times 2 = 88$; $\frac{1}{4}$ of the sheep are male; $88 \div 4 = 22$ sheep that are white and male)

  5 There are 33 black, female sheep. ($\frac{1}{3}$ of the sheep are black; $132 \div 3 = 44$; $\frac{3}{4}$ of the sheep are female; $44 \div 4 \times 3 = 33$ sheep that are black and female)

  6 Field 1 = 20, Field 2 = 40, Field 3 = 60. (Add together the ratios ($1 + 2 + 3 = 6$) and divide this number into the total number of lambs ($120 \div 6 = 20$). Then multiply this number with each of the ratios above. Field 1 has 20 lambs added (20×1); Field 2 has 40 lambs added (20×2) and Field 3 has 60 lambs added (20×3)).

Puzzle 4

(page 87)

Position	Country	Score
1st	Sweden	84
2nd	Iceland	76
3rd	Portugal	68
4th	France	65
5th	Italy	60
6th	England	56
7th	Spain	53
8th	Germany	40
9th	Poland	27
10th	Greece	19

Puzzle 5

(page 88)

Other examples are possible as long as each diagonal, row and column add up to the magic number.

8	1	6
3	5	7
4	9	2

13	12	17
18	14	10
11	16	15

−1	−2	3
4	0	−4
−3	2	1

Puzzle 6

(page 89)

Other pairs are possible as several fractions are equivalent to $\frac{1}{2}$, for example.

Fractions that add up to $\frac{2}{3}$:

$(\frac{1}{3} + \frac{2}{6})$ $(\frac{3}{9} + \frac{4}{12})$ $(\frac{1}{12} + \frac{7}{12})$

Fractions that add up to $\frac{5}{6}$:

$(\frac{4}{6} + \frac{1}{6})$ $(\frac{2}{12} + \frac{2}{3})$ $(\frac{5}{12} + \frac{5}{12})$

Fractions that add up to $\frac{7}{8}$:

$(\frac{1}{2} + \frac{3}{8})$ $(\frac{5}{8} + \frac{3}{12})$ $(\frac{1}{8} + \frac{3}{4})$

Fractions that add up to 1 whole:

$(\frac{6}{12} + \frac{2}{4})$ $(\frac{3}{6} + \frac{4}{8})$ $(\frac{8}{9} + \frac{1}{9})$

Fractions that add up to $1\frac{1}{2}$:

$(\frac{10}{12} + \frac{8}{12})$ $(\frac{6}{8} + \frac{9}{12})$ $(\frac{6}{9} + \frac{5}{6})$

Puzzle 7

(page 90)

Pyramid 1 – the operation is addition.

	3.10	
	1.74	1.36
0.91	0.83	0.53

Pyramid 2 – the operation is multiplication.

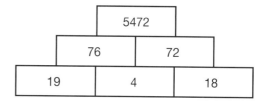

	5472	
	76	72
19	4	18

Pyramid 3 – the operation is multiplication.

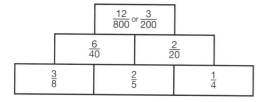

$\frac{12}{800}$ or $\frac{3}{200}$

$\frac{6}{40}$ $\frac{2}{20}$

$\frac{3}{8}$ $\frac{2}{5}$ $\frac{1}{4}$

Pyramid 4 – the operation is addition.

$1\frac{1}{9}$

$\frac{2}{3}$ $\frac{4}{9}$

$\frac{1}{3}$ $\frac{2}{6}$ $\frac{1}{9}$

Puzzle 8

(page 91)

1

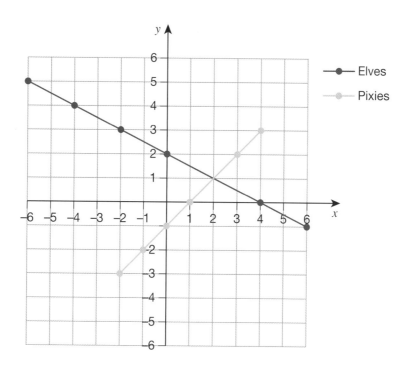

2

Elves	Coordinates	Pixies	Coordinates
Hefty	(−6, 5)	Hilby	(4, 3)
Nodkin	(−4, 4)	Lefty	(3, 2)
Hippy	(−2, 3)	Mully	(1, 0)
Russ	(0, 2)	Dippy	(0, −1)
Gully	(4, 0)	Bilbo	(−1, −2)
Muss	(6, −1)	Toggle	(−2, −3)

3 Bodkin and Boggle live at (2, 1)

Puzzle 9

(page 92)

To solve these riddles, use a process of elimination.

Two-digit square numbers are: 16, 25, 36, 49, 64, 81

The first digit is larger than the second: ~~16~~, ~~25~~, ~~36~~, ~~49~~, 64, 81

I am an even number: ~~16~~, ~~25~~, ~~36~~, ~~49~~, 64, ~~81~~

I must be 64.

Three-digit cube numbers are: 125, 216, 343, 512, 729

I am an odd number: 125, ~~216~~, 343, ~~512~~, 729

My first digit is 1: 125, ~~216~~, ~~343~~, ~~512~~, ~~729~~

I must be 125.

Two-digit prime numbers are: 11, 13, 17, 19, 23, 29, 31, 37, 41, 43, 47, 53, 59, 61, 67, 71, 73, 79, 83, 89, 97

My two digits add up to 16: ~~11, 13, 17, 19, 23, 29, 31, 37, 41, 43, 47, 53, 59, 61, 67, 71, 73~~, 79, ~~83, 89~~, 97

My first digit is smaller than my second.

I must be 79.

Puzzle 10

(page 93)

Task 1

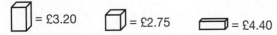

£1.65 (£4.40 − £2.75 = £1.65)

Task 2

8:45 (8:10 + 8 minutes = 8:18; 8:18 + 24 minutes = 8:42; 8:42 + 3 minutes = 8:45)

Task 3

1.86 kg (4.32 kg = 4320 g; add up the biscuits, coffee, marmalade and flour (2460 g) and subtract this from the total mass of the shopping (4320 − 2460 = 1860 g or 1.86 kg))

Test time: 0   5   10 minutes

Charlotte has a bag of sweets.

25% of the sweets are fizzy fruits.

$\frac{2}{5}$ of the sweets are candy canes.

30% are mints and the rest are toffees.

There are 13 toffees.

6 How many sweets are fizzy fruits? _____ ☐ 1

7 How many sweets are candy canes? _____ ☐ 1

8 How many sweets are mints? _____ ☐ 1

Danni is making fluffy animals for the school fair.

To make ten sheep she needs three balls of black wool and one ball of white wool.

To make ten dogs she needs five balls of brown wool and one ball of black wool.

To make ten polar bears she needs eight balls of white wool and $\frac{1}{4}$ ball of black wool.

Underline the correct answer for each question.

9 Danni has 84 balls of black wool. What is the maximum number of sheep Danni can make?

   a 14   **b** 28   **c** 86   **d** 280   **e** 320

10 Danni wants to make 25 dogs. How many balls of brown wool will she need?

   a $6\frac{1}{4}$ **b** $12\frac{1}{2}$ **c** 15   **d** 100   **e** 125

11 Danni wants to make 40 polar bears. How many balls of black wool does she need? ☐ 1

   a 1   **b** 2   **c** 3   **d** 4   **e** 5

12 Danni has a total of 50 balls of white wool. What is the maximum number of polar bears that Danni can make?

   a 6   **b** 16   **c** 60   **d** 62   **e** 600

Time for a break! ★ Go to Puzzle Page 89 →   Total ☐ 12

Test 19

Ashford School have completed a survey to find out which year group has read the most books and whether boys or girls have read the most. Use the bar chart of their results to answer the following questions.

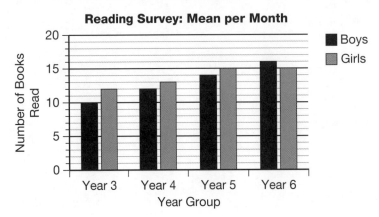

1 Michael says, "Girls read more books than boys in every year."

Is he correct? _____ ▢ 1

How do you know? _____ ▢ 1

2 Jodie says, "Children in Years 5 and 6 read more books than children in Years 3 and 4."

Is she correct? _____ ▢ 1

How do you know? _____ ▢ 1

3 Work out the mean number of books read by each year group. What is the difference between the year group with the lowest mean and the year group with the highest mean? _____ ▢ 1

Marianne bakes party cakes. She works out how large a cake should be when she knows how many portions are needed (one portion per guest).

She uses the formula $2p + 8 = s$ where p stands for the number of portions needed and s stands for the size of cake in centimetres cubed. Underline the correct answer for each question.

4 One customer is looking for a children's birthday cake for 12 guests. How large will the cake be? ▢ 1

a $12\,cm^3$ b $20\,cm^3$ c $24\,cm^3$ d $32\,cm^3$ e $40\,cm^3$

5 One customer is looking for a wedding cake for 85 guests. How large will the cake be?

a 85 cm³   **b** 93 cm³   **c** 178 cm³   **d** 186 cm³   **e** 210 cm³

6 Marianne has made an anniversary cake that is 420 cm³. How many guests has she catered for?

a 52   **b** 168   **c** 202   **d** 206   **e** 848

Ryan wants you to try to read his mind.

7 He says, "I am thinking of a number. It is a square number and a cube number. It has two digits."

What number do you think Ryan is thinking of?   _____

8 Ryan then says, "I am thinking about two numbers. Added together they make 728. The difference between them is 8."

What two numbers is Ryan thinking of?   _____

Rachel has programmed a maths app. For every number that she enters into the app, the programme will multiply it by three, then add seven to that number and then double this number to find a total. It also has a stopwatch counting down 60 seconds. The challenge is to work out the answer before the app does.

9 Rachel enters the number 13.

What answer will the app show?   _____

10 Rachel enters the number 21.

What answer will the app show?   _____

11 Rachel enters the number 34.

What answer will the app show?   _____

Total   13

Test 20

Mrs Cherry is baking a show-stopping plate of cheese sticks. Use this list of ingredients to answer the following questions. Underline the correct answer for each question.

Cheese sticks (makes 50)

150 g flour
50 g sesame seeds
200 g strong cheese
150 g butter
1 egg
1 pinch of paprika

1   Mrs Cherry wants to bake 175 cheese sticks. How much butter will she need?   `1`

   a   200 g   **b**   300 g   **c**   325 g   **d**   475 g   **e**   525 g

2   Mrs Cherry only has 40 g of strong cheese. How many cheese sticks can she make?   `1`

   a   10   **b**   12   **c**   15   **d**   20   **e**   25

> *Calculating Proportions Tip!*
> Sometimes it will not be a simple case of multiplying up or dividing down. Sometimes you might need to do more than one step, for example, divide by 3 then multiply by 4.

Juliet has bought a present that is in a box that is 40 cm long, 35 cm wide and 50 cm tall. She wants to wrap it up in some paper that is 2 m long and 1.5 m wide.

3   What is the volume of Juliet's box?   _____

4   What is the surface area of the box?   _____ 

5   Does Juliet have enough paper to wrap the present?   _____

Yanick is delivering flyers. There are 14 roads with the same number of houses in each. Yanick has enough flyers for every house to have one and he has a total of 658 flyers. He can deliver 120 flyers every hour. Underline the correct answer for each question.

6 How many houses are there are in each road?

a 14   b 28   c 47   d 56   e 120

7 How many flyers per minute can Yanick deliver?

a 2   b 3   c 4   d 15   e 20

8 How long will it take Yanick to deliver all of his flyers?

a 5h 20min   b 5h 29min   c 5h 33min   d 5h 45min   e 5h 48min

9 Yanick is paid 1p for each of the first 100 flyers and 2p for each of the next 100 flyers. He is paid 3p for each of the next 100 flyers and 4p for each of the next 100 flyers. This pattern continues. How much does Yanick earn for delivering all 658 of his flyers?

a £21.00   b £21.58   c £25.06   d £26.80   e £28.58

There are 20 pencils in a box and there are 125 boxes in a carton. There are 12 cartons to a pallet and Mr Sharp's Stationery Shop buys one pallet. The cost of a pallet is £900 and Mr Sharp sells the pencils for 27p each.

10 How many pencils does Mr Sharp buy? _____

11 How many pencils does Mr Sharp need to sell before he makes any profit? _____

12 If Mr Sharp sells all of his pencils, how much profit does he make in total? _____

13 Mr Sharp sells half of his pencils at 27p each and then he sells the other half in the sale at 25p each. How much profit does Mr Sharp now make once he has taken off the original cost of the pencils? _____

Total 13

Tubes of paint need to be mixed with water in the ratio 2:5.

Rosalind has six tubes of paint that are 33 ml each.

1 How much water does Rosalind need to mix all the tubes of paint? _____ ☐ 1

2 Rosalind has a new set of paint tubes and she uses approximately one litre of water.

How many millilitres of paint has Rosalind used? _____ ☐ 1

Brookside School is making an eating plan for school lunches. They draw a pie chart showing the proportion for each food group they want to include. Use the pie chart to answer the following questions. Underline the correct answer for each question.

Healthy Food Plan

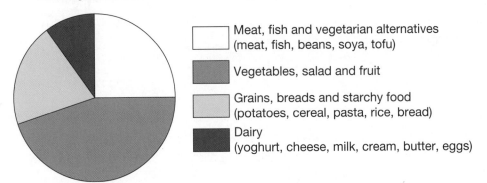

☐ Meat, fish and vegetarian alternatives
(meat, fish, beans, soya, tofu)

◼ Vegetables, salad and fruit

☐ Grains, breads and starchy food
(potatoes, cereal, pasta, rice, bread)

◼ Dairy
(yoghurt, cheese, milk, cream, butter, eggs)

3 What proportion of the plan should be made up of dairy products? ☐ 1

   a 2%   **b** 5%   **c** 10%   **d** 75%   **e** 90%

4 What proportion of the healthy plan should be made up of vegetables, salad and fruit? ☐ 1

   a 10%   **b** 20%   **c** 33%   **d** 45%   **e** 50%

5 How many degrees does the 'Meat, fish and vegetarian alternatives' sector represent? ☐ 1

   a 45°   **b** 75°   **c** 90°   **d** 180°   **e** 200°

There is an annual sale in the Home department. Customers get 5% off when they spend £20, they get 10% off when they spend £40 and they get 20% off when they spend £60 or more.

6 Spencer buys three cake tins and an icing kit. The tins are £6 each and the icing kit is £5.

How much does Spencer actually pay? _____ 1

7 Sam buys four towels and a travel case. The towels are £8 each and the travel case is £36.

How much does Sam actually pay? _____ 1

8 Loren buys a kettle which costs £24 and a toaster which costs £28.

How much change does she get from £60? _____ 1

In Mrs Fletcher's toy shop, Alfie works out how many pencil crayons and how many colouring books he can afford to buy. He works out that he can buy five crayons and three books for £3.25 or he can buy 15 crayons and one book for £4.55.
He writes these down like this: $5c + 3b = £3.25$ $15c + b = £4.55$

9 How much is one book? _____ 1

10 How much is one crayon? _____ 1

Reuben is one quarter of his mother's age. His brother Ben is one ninth of his father's age. Reuben is 5 years older than Ben and Ben is 3 years older than their little sister Sushi, who is about to start nursery. Their father is 5 years older than their mother.

11 How old is Reuben? _____ 1

12 How old is their father? _____ 1

13 How old is Sushi? _____ 1

Calculating Tip!
Begin with what you know. Sushi is about to start nursery, so she must be 1, 2, 3 or 4.

Total 13

Test 22

Simeon has some gem stones. The quartz stone is 28 g, the amethyst is 47 g, the jasper is 63 g and the amber is 15 g. The garnet is 104 g, the opal is 20 g and the topaz is 83 g. Simeon puts the stones in order, lightest first. Underline the correct answer for each question.

1 What is the approximate mean mass of the gem stones?

    a 36 g   **b** 51 g   **c** 60 g   **d** 72 g   **e** 104 g

2 Find the range of the stones' masses.

    a 47 g   **b** 55 g   **c** 63 g   **d** 84 g   **e** 89 g

Here is a distance chart between the sun and each of the planets in the Kaspakov galaxy. Use the chart to answer the following questions.

Planet	Distance from the Kaspakov Sun
Eoneus	8 354 612 km
Izo	912 779 km
Hask	12 788 314 km
Platipus	978 675 642 000 km
Tito	4 938 201 km

3 How far is Eoneus from the Kaspakov sun to the nearest ten thousand kilometres? _____

4 How much further from the Kaspakov sun is Platipus than Izo? _____

5 How far is Hask from the Kaspakov sun to the nearest hundred thousand kilometres? _____

The Woodland Fun Park is being constructed. The huge car parking area forms a square with each side 0.75 kilometres long. Each car park space is 2.7 metres wide and 12.2 metres long, which gives enough space for each car to drive in and out of the car park. Underline the correct answer for each question.

6 What is the area of the Woodland Fun Park car park?

 a $3\,m^2$ b $1500\,m^2$ c $3000\,m^2$ d $300\,000\,m^2$ e $562\,500\,m^2$

7 What is the maximum number of cars that can be parked at the Woodland Fun Park car park?

 a 61 b 750 c 811 d 16 897 e 33 794

8 It is expected that most weekends the car park will be 85% full.

How many cars are likely to be parked at the weekend?

 a 52 b 2535 c 14 362 d 28 725 e 1 436 245

Zara is setting up a Make a Mini Monster business. She makes 220 mini monsters.
Every 4th mini monster has a green ribbon in its hair.
Every 5th mini monster has a silver antenna on its head.
Every 9th mini monster has a purple curly tail.
Underline the correct answer for each question.

9 How many mini monsters have a green ribbon and a silver antenna?

 a 5 b 11 c 44 d 55 e 66

10 How many mini monsters have a silver antenna and a purple curly tail?

 a 4 b 5 c 11 d 44 e 55

11 How many mini monsters have a green ribbon and a silver antenna and a purple curly tail?

 a 55 b 11 c 4 d 2 e 1

Total 11

Test 23

There is a large queue outside the cinema on Friday evening for the new film. Alice, Rose and Emily are excited to see it. Underline the correct answer for each question.

1 Alice counts 57 people in front of her in the queue. She also works out that she is $\frac{3}{4}$ of the way from the front of the queue. How many people in total are in the queue?

    a 76   **b** 114   **c** 157   **d** 171   **e** 228

2 Rose opens her bag of sweets after 24 minutes. She has watched 20% of the film. How long does the film last?

    a 60 min   **b** 75 min   **c** 90 min   **d** 120 min   **e** 280 min

3 The film begins at 17:40 and Emily starts to eat her popcorn. She finishes her popcorn at 18:10. What percentage of the film does Emily spend eating her popcorn?

    a 20%   **b** 25%   **c** 30%   **d** 40%   **e** 50%

Samuel is making bead monsters. He uses two red beads, three white beads and four striped beads for each monster.

4 Samuel wants to make 12 monsters. How many red, white and striped beads does he need? Fill in the numbers.

    red beads = _____   white beads = _____   striped beads = _____

5 Samuel wants to make 35 monsters. He has 100 red beads, 120 white beads and 135 striped beads.

    Does Samuel have enough beads to make 35 monsters? _____

6 Red beads cost 13p each, white beads cost 17p each and striped beads cost 23p each. Samuel wants to make 120 monsters.

    How much will the beads cost in total? _____

The greengrocer is weighing out some vegetables to make up soup kits.
Use the information he has given to answer the following questions.
Underline the correct answer for each question.

	Onion Soup	Parsnip Soup
	5 onions	1 onion
	1 parsnip	4 parsnips
Mass:	680 g	440 g

7 What is the mass of one parsnip?

a 50 g   b 70 g   c 80 g   d 88 g   e 100 g

8 What is the mass of one onion?

a 116 g   b 120 g   c 122 g   d 124 g   e 126 g

Rose and Alice both have some cards with a single-digit number on each. Rose and Alice pair one card with another. Rose squares the number on the first card. Alice cubes the number on the second card. They place these answers together to make a code.

9 Which two numbers make the code 8127? _____

10 Which two numbers make the code 4964? _____

11 Which two numbers make the code 6408? _____

12 Which two numbers make the code 3601? _____

Total   12

Test 24

0   5   10 minutes

Test time: 0   5   10 minutes

Samira, Emi and Vaz are sharing some coloured pens in the ratio $1:2:3$. Samira notices that the number of pens in one pile is a square number, the number of pens in another pile is a cube number and the number of pens in each pile is an even number. The three piles of coloured pens, added together, come to a number less than 40.

1   How many coloured pens does Samira have?   _____   ☐ 1

2   How many coloured pens does Emi have?   _____   ☐ 1

3   How many coloured pens does Vaz have?   _____   ☐ 1

Logic Tip!

To solve this type of question, look at the information to find a logical place to start. For example, here you need to look at numbers less than 40 that are squared even numbers and cubed even numbers. Once you have found the sets of suitable numbers, you can then use ratio to find the exact numbers.

My map has a scale of $1:80\,000$.

Underline the correct answer for each question.

4   I walk from my home to the doctors' surgery which is a journey of 1.6 km. How many centimetres on the map is this?   ☐ 1

     a   0.75 cm   **b**   0.8 cm   **c**   1 cm   **d**   2 cm   **e**   2.5 cm

5   I then walk from the doctors' surgery to the shop which is 0.75 cm on the map. How far is this for me to walk?   ☐ 1

     a   200 m   **b**   600 m   **c**   750 m   **d**   7500 m   **e**   1000 m

© 2017 Oxford University Press • COPYING STRICTLY PROHIBITED

Rhiannon buys jewellery at car boot sales and then sells it online. She makes a table of what she has bought and sold over the last month so that she can work out how much profit she has made. Use her table to answer the following questions. Underline the correct answer for each question.

Item	Bought For	Sold At
Rings	£6.23	£15.25
Necklaces	£8.50	£11.90
Bracelets	£4.00	£11.20
Hair clips	£7.30	£6.57
Brooches	£3.97	£46.30

6 Which item did Rhiannon make the most profit with?

a Rings **b** Necklaces **c** Bracelets **d** Hair clips **e** Brooches

7 Rhiannon made 40% profit on which item?

a Rings **b** Necklaces **c** Bracelets **d** Hair clips **e** Brooches

8 Rhiannon made a loss on hair clips. What percentage did she lose?

a 5% **b** 10% **c** 15% **d** 20% **e** 25%

Mr Ramsay sells packets of batteries in his shop. There are 24 packets of batteries in each box and there are 36 boxes in a pallet. Mr Ramsay buys three pallets. He pays £648 for each pallet. He sells a packet of batteries for £1.80.

9 How many packets of batteries does Mr Ramsay buy? _____

10 How many packets of batteries does Mr Ramsay have to sell before he is able to make a profit? _____

11 Mr Ramsay sells all of his batteries. How much is his total profit? _____

12 A customer buys a box full of batteries and asks for a 15% discount. How much does he pay in total? _____

Total 12

Test 25

Megan is making gift hampers to sell. Here is the pricing that she is using:

A fruit package, which is expressed as f, costs £4.75.

A chocolate package, which is expressed as c, costs £8.99.

A pack of balloons, which is expressed as b, costs £2.20.

The cost of the hamper and wrapping, which is expressed as h, is £3.75.

Underline the correct answer for each question.

1   Mrs Crossfield places an order that Megan writes down as $2f + c + h$.

How much does Mrs Crossfield's order come to?

   a   £21.42   **b**   £21.24   **c**   £22.24   **d**   £24.22   **e**   £24.42

2   Mr Walker places an order that Megan writes down as $f + c + b + h$.

Mr Walker pays with a £20 note. How much change does he receive?

   a   £3.51   **b**   £2.51   **c**   £1.51   **d**   51p   **e**   31p

3   Janice places an order that Megan writes down as $2(f + c) + h$.

Janice pays with £40. How much change does she receive?

   a   £3.41   **b**   £8.77   **c**   £10.24   **d**   £15.23   **e**   £17.49

Abinaath has made a robot that he can move around the table. Each step the robot makes is exactly the same size. Abinaath gives the following instructions where N is north, E is east, S is south and W is west. Underline the correct answer for each question.

4   N4, E5, N3, W7, S7

Which direction is needed for the robot to return to its starting position?

   a   E1   **b**   E2   **c**   W1   **d**   W2   **e**   S1

5   S5, W2, N5, E4, N2, W2

Which direction is needed for the robot to return to its starting position?

a E2   **b** N1   **c** W2   **d** E1   **e** S2

Directional Tip!

An easy way of solving this question type is to hand-draw a quick grid. Beginning on any central square, you can then follow the robot directions and find the answer. If you need more grid squares, simply add them as you go.

Class 6H are looking at the temperature of water in three containers. Their teacher pours the same amount of boiling water into a tall tube, a cereal bowl and a tray. The class then record the temperature over 20 minutes. Use the graph of their results to answer the following questions.

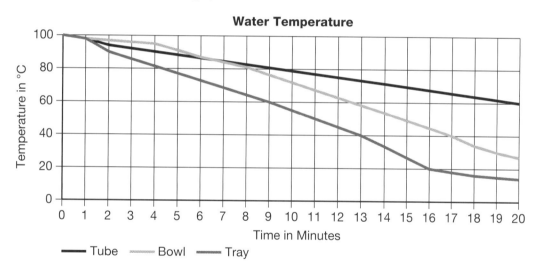

6   After how many minutes was the water in the tray at 40 °C?   _____

7   After 17 minutes, what was the temperature of the water in the bowl?   _____

8   How much longer did it take the water in the tube to reach 60 °C than the water in the tray?   _____

Total   8

Test 26

Fred has nine keys that are numbered from 1 to 9. To create a code, he picks two keys. He adds the number on each of these keys and writes down the answer. Then he multiplies the number on each of these keys and writes down the answer on the right of his first answer, making a four-digit code.

1 Which two numbers has he added together and then multiplied together to make the code 1024?   _____   1

2 Which two numbers has he added together and then multiplied together to make the code 1556?   _____   1

3 Which two numbers has he added together and then multiplied together to make the code 1118?   _____   1

The pupils in Class 6H grew some sunflowers and measured their heights after 10 weeks. They drew a bar chart of their results. Use the bar chart to answer the following questions.

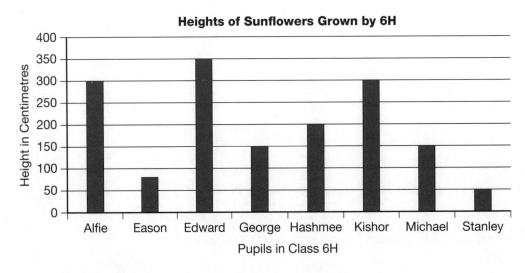

Heights of Sunflowers Grown by 6H

4 What is the difference in height between the shortest and the tallest sunflowers?   _____   1

5 What is the median height of the sunflowers?   _____   1

There are 1.6 kilometres in 1 mile. Travelling from Nelson to Scarborough is 100 miles. I left the house at 12:30 p.m. and I have driven 68 miles of the way. It has taken me 1 hour and 45 minutes. Underline the correct answer for each question.

6 How many kilometres is the journey from Nelson to Scarborough?

a 62.5 km   b 85 km   c 160 km   d 210 km   e 320 km

7 What percentage of the journey have I got left to drive?

a 32%   b 42%   c 66%   d 68%   e 86%

8 If I drive at the same speed all the way, what time will I reach Scarborough?

a 1:35 p.m.   b 2:34 p.m.   c 3:04 p.m.   d 3:35 p.m.   e 4:10 p.m.

Ellie has a map with a scale of 1 : 720 000.
Underline the correct answer for each question.

9 Ellie is going to her cheerleading class. She has to travel 3.6 km to get there. How many centimetres is this on the map?

a 0.25 cm   b 0.5 cm   c 1 cm   d 2.5 cm   e 3.6 cm

10 Ellie is planning a walk at the weekend. She finds a trail that measures 1.5 cm on the map. How long will her walk be?

a 15 km   b 14.4 km   c 10.8 km   d 10 km   e 9.2 km

11 At the weekend Ellie begins her walk. She stops for a break when she has walked $\frac{1}{3}$ of the way. How far has she walked before she stops for her break?

a 3.6 km   b 3.5 km   c 3.4 km   d 3.3 km   e 3.0 km

12 Ellie is going on holiday with her family. She is travelling 108 km. How many centimetres would this be on the map?

a 0.15 cm   b 1.5 cm   c 15 cm   d 150 cm   e 1500 cm

Total   12

Test 27

The pupils in Years 4, 5 and 6 at Ivanhoe Street School were surveyed to find out what type of book they preferred to read.

1   In Year 4, the most popular type of book was cartoon books, which were preferred by 30% of the year group. 24 children chose cartoon books.

How many children are in Year 4?   _____   ◯ 1

2   In Year 5, the most popular type of book was animal stories, which 27 pupils chose. This was $\frac{3}{5}$ of the year group.

How many children are in Year 5?   _____   ◯ 1

3   There were 21 children in Year 6 who chose adventure books. This was chosen by a quarter of the year group.

How many pupils in total were in the survey?   _____   ◯ 1

A garden centre buys solar fountains to sell. There are four solar fountains to every box and there are five boxes in a carton. There are six cartons to a pallet and the garden centre buys two pallets. Each pallet costs £2700 and each solar fountain in the garden centre has a price of £75. Underline the correct answer for each question.

4   How many solar fountains have to be sold before the garden centre begins to make a profit?   ◯ 1

   a 36   **b** 45   **c** 65   **d** 72   **e** 84

5   If the garden centre sold every solar fountain, how much profit would they make after they had taken away the initial cost of the fountains?   ◯ 1

   a £440   **b** £6300   **c** £9000   **d** £12 600   **e** £36 000

6   The garden centre sells half of the solar fountains at full price and the remaining half with a '10% off' sale price.

How much profit does the garden centre make after they have taken away the initial cost of the fountains?   ◯ 1

   a £5850   **b** £8100   **c** £11 700   **d** £16 200   **e** £18 620

Brandon has 120 new stickers. Every 4th sticker is a special edition. Every 5th sticker is one Brandon already has. Underline the correct answer for each question.

7 How many stickers are copies of ones that Brandon already has?

   a 24   **b** 25   **c** 50   **d** 75   **e** 96

8 How many stickers are copies that Brandon already has and are special edition stickers?

   a 5   **b** 6   **c** 40   **d** 96   **e** 114

Common Multiples Tip!

With this type of question, remember to divide the total to make a group and then subdivide that group to reflect all of the categories needed.

Leo uses a 3D printer to make figures that he sells. He makes a table of how much each figure costs and how much he has sold it for. He can then work out how much profit he has made. Use his table to answer the following questions. Underline the correct answer for each question.

Figure Name	Spaceman	Hippie	Punk	Skater	Zombie
Cost to Make	£8.94	£7.25	£6.80	£9.79	£7.25
Price Sold	£30.50	£26.40	£18.15	£32.80	£21.75

9 How much profit did Leo make with his Spaceman figure?

   a £8.94   **b** £21.56   **c** £20.56   **d** £21.65   **e** £30.50

10 Which item did Leo make the most profit with?

   a Spaceman   **b** Hippie   **c** Punk   **d** Skater   **e** Zombie

11 Leo made a 200% profit on which figure?

   a Spaceman   **b** Hippie   **c** Punk   **d** Skater   **e** Zombie

Total 11

Jayden has a 2 cm cube and a larger box that is a 4 cm cube. Underline the correct answer for each question.

1   What is the volume of Jayden's 2 cm cube?

   a $4 \, cm^3$ **b** $8 \, cm^3$ **c** $16 \, cm^3$ **d** $36 \, cm^3$ **e** $216 \, cm^3$

2   What is the surface area of his 2 cm cube?

   a $6 \, cm^2$ **b** $16 \, cm^2$ **c** $20 \, cm^2$ **d** $24 \, cm^2$ **e** $36 \, cm^2$

3   Jayden places the 2 cm cube inside the larger box. What fraction of the volume of larger box does the cube take up?

   a $\frac{1}{8}$ **b** $\frac{1}{5}$ **c** $\frac{1}{4}$ **d** $\frac{1}{3}$ **e** $\frac{1}{2}$

4   If Jayden places the 2 cm cube into the larger box, how much space is left in the larger box?

   a $8 \, cm^3$ **b** $16 \, cm^3$ **c** $32 \, cm^3$ **d** $56 \, cm^3$ **e** $60 \, cm^3$

At the sewing club, Alex is making a coat. The pattern Alex is using has a scale of 1 : 4.

5   The length of the coat is 64 cm.

   How many centimetres is this on the pattern?   _____

6   The length of the sleeve on the pattern is 21 cm.

   How many centimetres is this in reality?   _____

7   Alex is adding square pockets to the coat. Each side of the pockets measures 24 cm.

   What will this be on the pattern?   _____

Football shirts cost £38.99 plus £2.25 for each letter on the back. The formula for this is $2.25n + 38.99$, where n is the number of letters on the back and 38.99 is the cost of the football shirt.

8 Sam wants his name on the back of his shirt.

How much does he pay? _____ ◯ 1

9 Betina wants her name on the back of her shirt. She pays with three £20 notes.

How much change does she receive? _____ ◯ 1

10 Fitzgerald wants his name on the back of his shirt. He has the same amount of money as Betina.

Does he have enough? _____ ◯ 1

Year 6 collected some giant snails for their science project. They measured the length and the height of each giant snail. Use the table of their results to answer the following questions. Underline the correct answer for each question.

Snail	Length	Height
Alf	20 cm	7 cm
Bert	18 cm	8 cm
Cecil	17 cm	5 cm
Duncan	19 cm	6 cm
Eric	16 cm	7 cm

11 What is the mean length of the snails? ◯ 1

    a 16 cm   **b** 17 cm   **c** 18 cm   **d** 19 cm   **e** 20 cm

12 Which snail has the smallest difference between its length and its height? ◯ 1

    a Alf   **b** Bert   **c** Cecil   **d** Duncan   **e** Eric

13 Find the range of the snails' lengths. ◯ 1

    a 1 cm   **b** 2 cm   **c** 3 cm   **d** 4 cm   **e** 5 cm

Total ☐ 13

Test 29

At the car manufacturer, there are 22 cars parked one behind the other. Each car measures 430 cm and there is 0.5 m between each parked car. Each car will be sold for £19 250.

1   How long is the line of cars?   _____ 

2   How much in total is the line of cars worth?   _____

The reindeer feeding guide shows the optimum mass of food that a reindeer should be fed based on its height. Use the graph to answer the following questions.

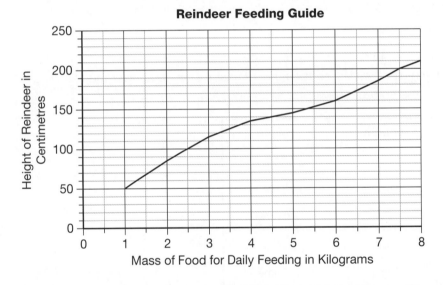

3   Rudolph the reindeer is 1 m tall.

    What mass of food does he need each day?   _____

4   Comet the reindeer eats 42 kg of food each week.

    How tall is Comet?   _____

5   Blitzen the reindeer is 2 m tall. He is going away for the month of December.

    How much food will Blitzen need to take with him?   _____ 

Here is a diagram of Menden village. Each square is 100 m × 100 m. Use the diagram to answer the following questions. Underline the correct answer for each question.

6 I walk from the school to the Recycling Centre.

What directions do I take?

a E, N   b N, W   c E, S   d E   e N

7 I travel 400 m south from the doctors' and then 200 m east.

Where do I end up?

a Office   b School   c Vets'   d Café   e Recycling Centre

8 From the café I travel 500 m north and then 100 m west.

Where do I end up?

a Doctors'   b Church   c Office   d Recycling Centre   e Vets'

Total 8

Test 30

Malachi has weighed different combinations of shapes like this:

 = 493 g   = 561 g

 = 551 g   ⬤▲⬤ = 657 g

1 What is the mass of one white diamond?   _____   ⬭ 1

2 What is the mass of one black circle?   _____   ⬭ 1

3 What is the mass of one grey triangle?   _____   ⬭ 1

Schwartz crosses the winning line in 9th place at exactly the same time as three other cars. There were 52 cars that began the race. Underline the correct answer for each question.

4 How many cars did Schwartz beat?   ⬭ 1

   a 5   **b** 6   **c** 40   **d** 96   **e** 114

5 What fraction of the total cars in the race came equal or better than Schwartz?   ⬭ 1

   a $\frac{9}{52}$ **b** $\frac{7}{26}$ **c** $\frac{3}{13}$ **d** $\frac{11}{52}$ **e** $\frac{5}{26}$

Mr Dylan is going to buy five tins of paint. He sees the paint he wants in three shops and each shop offers a different deal. Use the information on the posters to answer the following questions. Underline the correct answer for each question.

Paints-4-U
Paint £16 a tin
15% off all purchases

Rainbow Paints
Paint £20 a tin
Buy 3 and only pay for 2!

6 What is the most expensive price for five tins of paint?   ⬭ 1

   a £84   **b** £80   **c** £74   **d** £70   **e** £68

7 What is the cheapest price for five tins of paint?

    a £84   **b** £80   **c** £74   **d** £70   **e** £68

8 Mr Dylan decides to buy six tins of paint.

Which is the cheapest price for six tins of paint?

    a £84   **b** £81.60   **c** £80.40   **d** £80   **e** £78.20

Here is a diagram of Corfton Village. Each square of the grid represents 100 metres long and 100 metres wide. Use the grid to answer the following questions. Underline the correct answer for each question.

Duck Pond	School	Church	Hotel
Florists'			Chemist
Grocers'			Doctors'
Post Office			Café
Woods	Butchers'	Bakery	Chip Shop

N ↑

9 I come out of the butchers' and walk 200 m north and 200 m east. Where am I?

    a Chemist   **b** Doctors'   **c** Café   **d** Florists'   **e** Grocers'

10 I come out of the Post Office and walk 100 m east, 300 m north and then 200 m east. Where am I?

    a Florists'   **b** Duck Pond   **c** School   **d** Church   **e** Hotel

11 I come out of the school and walk 200 m south, then 100 m west, then finally 200 m south. Where am I?

    a Post Office   **b** Woods   **c** Butchers'   **d** Grocers'   **e** Café

Total   11

Puzzle 1 — Message in a Bottle

Sian has found a message in a bottle, but the paper just has lots of numbers written in a grid and some calculations.

Solve the calculations. Then colour in the grid to see what the message is.

a $0.6508 + 0.3492 =$ _____

b $2^2 =$ _____

c The 4th prime number is _____

d $2\frac{3}{4} \div \frac{1}{4} =$ _____

e $50 \times 0.28 =$ _____

f $392.6 \div 39.26 =$ _____

g $14\frac{3}{8} + 2\frac{10}{16} =$ _____

h $4328 \times 0 =$ _____

Now colour in every square that has these numbers in them.

10	12	8	0	15	9	6	5	3	11	19	14	20	2	6	19	20	16
4	2	13	17	16	5	2	9	15	17	5	7	6	16	9	3	15	12
17	15	5	11	2	3	13	5	2	10	8	17	2	3	2	13	6	2
1	11	14	4	13	1	17	4	16	4	2	1	2	17	17	0	10	11
0	4	10	7	8	10	6	4	2	1	9	4	16	11	16	18	5	10
11	3	9	1	2	0	1	14	13	14	3	7	12	14	9	2	13	4
14	12	2	14	6	7	8	5	6	7	16	10	3	14	15	12	9	7
4	5	8	7	3	11	3	7	12	10	2	4	13	11	3	8	2	14
17	3	6	10	12	14	14	10	5	4	6	4	5	4	11	7	14	10

What is the word that you have revealed? _____

Puzzle 2

Wedding Day

1   There is a wedding today. As the guests arrive at the venue, they sit on both sides of the aisle. There are 32 rows of seats on each side of the aisle and each row contains 8 seats.

If 75% of the seats are taken, how many guests are at the venue?

_____

2   The bride has a beautiful bouquet of flowers. There are red roses making up 25% of the bouquet with white roses making up $\frac{2}{5}$. Pink, scented carnations make up 10% of the bouquet and the remaining flowers are lilies. There are 8 pink, scented carnations.

Complete the sentence:

There are _____ red roses, _____ white roses and

_____ lilies.

3   As the guests leave the wedding venue, the two families are introduced to each other. Twelve guests all shake hands with each other.

If they only shake hands with each other once, how many handshakes take place in total?

_____

4   The wedding venue has prepared 168 glasses of elderflower fizz for the guests to enjoy. This is made up of elderflower cordial and sparkling water in the ratio 1:6.

Each glass holds 250 ml of elderflower fizz.

How much sparkling water is needed?

_____

5   The wedding cake is made of three tiers. The top tier is 30 cm × 30 cm × 6 cm. The middle tier is 40 cm × 40 cm × 6 cm and the bottom tier is 50 cm × 50 cm × 6 cm.

What is the total volume of cake? _____

Puzzle 3

Farmer Frank

Farmer Frank has 132 sheep that need to go into three fields.

One in three sheep are black. The rest are white.

A quarter of the sheep, of both colours, are male.

50% of the sheep, of both colours, are lambs.

The number of sheep in Field 1 is three times more than the number of sheep in Field 2.

The number of sheep in Field 3 is seven times more than the number of sheep in Field 2.

1   How many sheep are in Field 1? _____

2   How many sheep are in Field 2? _____

3   How many sheep are in Field 3? _____

4   How many sheep are white males? _____

5   How many sheep are black females? _____

Farmer Frank now has another 120 lambs. They are divided between the three fields in the ratio 1 : 2 : 3.

6   How many lambs will be added to each field?

Field 1 = _____   Field 2 = _____   Field 3 = _____

Puzzle 4   Intervoice Competition

Here are the results from the Intervoice Competition. Add up the scores for each country and then place them on the leader board with the highest score first.

England	10, 3, 8, 0, 4, 2, 10, 9, 6, 4	_____
France	5, 4, 6, 8, 4, 8, 9, 9, 7, 5	_____
Germany	8, 0, 3, 0, 10, 4, 3, 7, 2, 3	_____
Italy	6, 7, 5, 8, 4, 9, 5, 6, 6, 4	_____
Poland	3, 4, 1, 2, 5, 3, 4, 1, 2, 2	_____
Sweden	10, 9, 10, 9, 8, 6, 10, 7, 7, 8	_____
Iceland	9, 7, 9, 8, 7, 9, 9, 5, 7, 6	_____
Greece	1, 0, 2, 1, 0, 3, 2, 4, 4, 2	_____
Spain	5, 4, 6, 3, 7, 2, 8, 7, 6, 5	_____
Portugal	7, 7, 6, 6, 8, 7, 6, 6, 7, 8	_____

Position	Country	Score
1st		
2nd		
3rd		
4th		
5th		
6th		
7th		
8th		
9th		
10th		

Puzzle 5

Here are some magic squares. In each magic square, every row, column and diagonal add up to the same number. Solve each magic square using the numbers given.

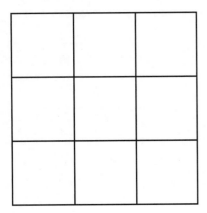

Using these numbers:

1, 2, 3, 4, 5, 6, 7, 8, 9

make every row, column and diagonal add up to **15**.

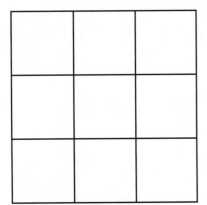

Using these numbers:

10, 11, 12, 13, 14, 15, 16, 17, 18

make every row, column and diagonal add up to **42**.

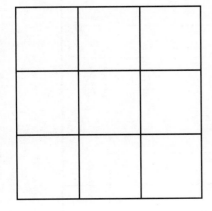

Using these numbers:

–4, –3, –2, –1, 0, 1, 2, 3, 4

make every row, column and diagonal add up to **0**.

Puzzle 6

Fraction Friends

Find pairs of fractions that add up to the totals shown in the stars. Each total has three pairs of fractions. Use each fraction only once. One has been done for you.

$1\frac{1}{2}$

$\frac{2}{3}$

$\frac{1}{3}$ $\frac{5}{6}$ $\frac{2}{6}$ $\frac{6}{9}$ $\frac{5}{8}$

$\frac{4}{12}$ $\frac{4}{6}$ $\frac{1}{9}$ $\frac{1}{6}$ $\frac{8}{9}$

$\frac{5}{6}$

$\frac{3}{6}$ $\frac{2}{3}$ $\frac{1}{2}$ $\frac{3}{4}$ $\frac{3}{8}$

$\frac{1}{8}$ $\frac{6}{8}$ $\frac{3}{12}$ $\frac{6}{12}$ $\frac{5}{12}$

1 $\frac{2}{4}$ $\frac{5}{12}$ $\frac{2}{12}$ $\frac{4}{8}$ $\frac{10}{12}$

$\frac{7}{8}$

$\frac{7}{12}$ $\frac{8}{12}$ $\frac{1}{12}$ $\frac{3}{9}$ $\frac{9}{12}$

Puzzle 7

Number Pyramids

Here are some number pyramids. The number in each block of the pyramid has been calculated from the numbers in the two blocks below it. Fill in the missing numbers to complete each pyramid. You will need to work out what operator has been used in each pyramid.

Pyramid 1

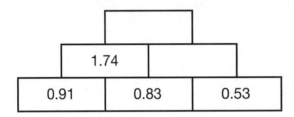

Pyramid 2

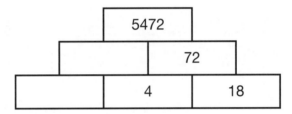

Pyramid 3

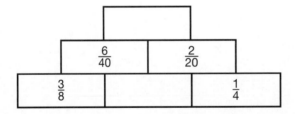

Pyramid 4

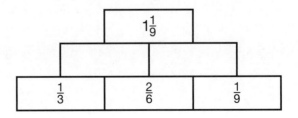

Puzzle 8   In the Land of the Elves and Pixies

Bodkin and the six other elves live on one path. Boggle and the other six pixies live on another path. Bodkin and Boggle live in the same house where the two paths cross. One of the elves has the furthest to travel to visit Bodkin and Boggle's house. The problem is this: the elves and pixies are all mixed up.

Here are their names and the coordinates of their houses:

Toggle (–2, –3)   Russ (0, 2)   Nodkin (–4, 4)   Muss (6, –1)

Mully (1, 0)   Lefty (3, 2)   Hippy (–2, 3)   Hilby (4, 3)

Hefty (–6, 5)   Gully (4, 0)   Dippy (0, –1)   Bilbo (–1, –2)

1 Plot the houses on the xy-coordinate grid. Then draw the two paths.

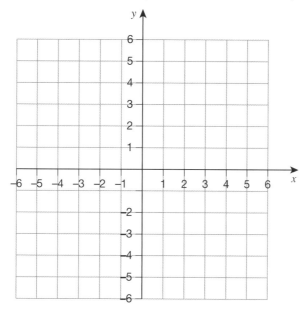

2 Work out who are the elves and who are the pixies.

Elves	Pixies
Bodkin	Boggle

3 What are the coordinates for where Boggle and Bodkin live? (___, ___)

Puzzle 9

What Number Am I?

I am a square number.

I am a two-digit number.

My first digit is larger than my second.

I am an even number.

What number am I?

_____

I am a cube number.

I am a three-digit number.

I am an odd number.

My first digit is '1'.

What number am I?

_____

I am a prime number.

I am a two-digit number.

My two digits add up to 16.

My first digit is smaller than my second.

What number am I?

_____

Puzzle 10

Time Challenge

Here is your challenge ... if you choose to accept it! Complete all three of these tasks in no more than 5 minutes. Can you do it?

Task 1

Work out how much each box is worth:

= £10.35   = £8.25   = £6.40

= _____   = _____   = _____

Now subtract the value of the the box worth the least from the value of the

box worth the most. _____

Task 2

Look at the following clock and read the information below:

Alex leaves the house at this time to get to school. It takes him 8 minutes to walk to the bus stop and he has a 24-minute bus journey, which stops right outside the school. Alex always has 3 minutes to get off the bus and into the playground before the school bell rings.

What time does the school bell ring? _____

Task 3

Louise has a bag full of shopping. The total mass of the bag of shopping is 4.32 kg. She takes out the biscuits with a mass of 455 g, the coffee with a mass of 225 g, the marmalade with a mass of 280 g and the flour with a mass of 1.5 kg.

What is the mass of the bag of remaining shopping? _____ kg

Did you meet the challenge successfully?
Check your answers and then add your name to
the badge.

....

is a
**TIME CHALLENGE
CHAMPION!**

Key words

algebra unknown quantities in a formula that are represented by letters: for example, if the price of an apple is a and the price of a pear is p, and two apples and three pears cost £2.20, this can be shown by the equation $2a + 3p = 2.20$

area the measurement of a surface: to find the area of a rectangle, multiply the length by the width; to find the area of a triangle, multiply half of the base by the height

BODMAS the order in which you do the operations in a calculation: Brackets, Order/Indices, Division, Multiplication, Addition, Subtraction

compass direction the direction a person or thing can move: for example *North, South, East* and *West*. From an arrow pointing **N** (north), work clockwise through **E** (east), **S** (south), **W** (west) and back to **N** (north). Each segment is a 90° turn

coordinates the two numbers that describe a point on a grid: for example, in (1, 4) the first coordinate is the horizontal distance along the x-axis and the second coordinate is vertical distance up the y-axis

cube number a number that is the result of a number being multiplied by itself and then multiplied by itself again: for example $3^3 = 3 \times 3 \times 3 = \underline{27}$

degrees and angles a full circle is 360°; a semicircle is 180°; a right angle is 90°

fraction part of a whole number: for example *a half* ($\frac{1}{2}$), which is $1 \div 2$

map scale the relationship between the distance on a map and the corresponding distance in reality: for example *1:50 000* means 1 cm on the map represents 50 000 cm in reality

mass the amount of matter in an object, measured in, for example, grams and kilograms. From Year 2, children are expected to use the term 'mass' rather than 'weight'

mean the average that is calculated by adding up all the values and dividing by the number of values

median the average found by ordering the values from smallest to largest and then selecting the middle value (or the mean of the middle two values)

negative number a value that is less than zero

percentage a number out of 100: for example *50 out of 100 is 50%*

perimeter the length of the outside edge of a shape

prime number any number that can only be divided by itself and 1, for example 2

probability the chance of an event happening, represented as a fraction or percentage: for example *the probability of flipping 'heads' on a coin is $\frac{1}{2}$ or 50%*

profit the sum of money remaining when costs have been deducted: for example *if I buy some books for £5 and sell them for £20, I make £15 profit*

proportion a part, share or number used to show how a whole is divided up; can be scaled up or down using the

Key words

same proportion: for example *if 100 g sugar makes 10 biscuits, then 200 g sugar makes 20 biscuits and 50 g sugar makes 5 biscuits* – the proportion does not change but the amount does

range found by subtracting the lowest value from the highest value

ratio shows the relative sizes of two or more values: for example *Tom, Tam and Tim share £12 in the ratio 1:2:3 (1 + 2 + 3 = 6) £12 ÷ 6 = £2 so Tom gets £2 (£2 × 1), Tam gets £4 (£2 × 2) and Tim gets £6 (£2 × 3)*

rounding if a number ends in 5 or higher, round up, otherwise round down; if rounding to the nearest 100, look at the value in the tens column; if rounding to the nearest 1000, look at the value in the hundreds column

square number the result of a number being multiplied by itself; for example $3^2 = 3 \times 3 = \underline{9}$

surface area the total area of the surface of a three-dimensional object: for example, for a cuboid, work out the area of the six faces and add them together, or a quick method is to find the area of the front, top and right side and then to double up for the back, bottom and left side

volume the amount of space occupied by a three-dimensional object: for example to find the volume of any cuboid, multiply the length by the width by the height

x-**axis** the horizontal axis line on a grid, where the numbers to the right of zero are positive numbers and the numbers to the left of zero are negative numbers

y-**axis** the vertical axis line on a grid, where the numbers above zero are positive numbers and the numbers below zero are negative numbers

Progress chart

How did you do? Fill in your score below and shade in the corresponding boxes to compare your progress across the different tests.

50%   100%   50%   100%

Test 1, p4 Score:___/11

Test 2, p6 Score:___/10

Test 3, p8 Score: ___/12

Test 4, p10 Score: ___/10

Test 5, p12 Score:___/12

Test 6, p14 Score:___/11

Test 7, p16 Score:___/12

Test 8, p18 Score: ___/12

Test 9, p20 Score: ___/10

Test 10, p22 Score:___/11

Test 11, p24 Score:___/8

Test 12, p26 Score:___/13

Test 13, p28 Score: ___/14

Test 14, p30 Score: ___/12

Test 15, p32 Score:___/12

Test 16, p34 Score:___/12

Test 17, p36 Score: ___/13

Test 18, p38 Score: ___/12

Test 19, p60 Score: ___/13

Test 20, p62 Score:___/13

Test 21, p64 Score:___/13

Test 22, p66 Score:___11

Test 23, p68 Score: ___/12

Test 24, p70 Score: ___/12

Test 25, p72 Score:___/8

Test 26, p74 Score:___/12

Test 27, p76 Score: ___/11

Test 28, p78 Score: ___/13

Test 29, p80 Score: ___/8

Test 30, p82 Score:___/11